*The ABCs of Making*

# TEDDY BEARS

# The ABCs of Making

# TEDDY BEARS

### LINDA MEAD

*Martingale*
& COMPANY

CREDITS

President . . . . . . . . Nancy J. Martin
CEO . . . . . . . . . . . . Daniel J. Martin
Publisher . . . . . . . . . . Jane Hamada
Editorial Director . . . Mary V. Green
Design and Production Manager . . .
Stan Green
Editorial Project Manager . . . . . . . .
Tina Cook
Technical Editor . . . . . Ursula Reikes
Copy Editor . . . . . . . . Ellen Balstad
Illustrators . . . . . . . . . . . . . . . . . . .
Robin Strobel, Laurel Strand
Photographer . . . . . . . . . Brent Kane
Cover and Text Designer . . . . . . . .
Trina Stahl

*Martingale*
& COMPANY

The ABCs of Making Teddy Bears
© 2000 by Linda Mead

Martingale & Company
20205 144th Ave NE
Woodinville, WA 98072-8478 USA
www.martingale-pub.com

Printed in Hong Kong
05 04 03 02          6 5 4 3 2

MISSION STATEMENT

*We are dedicated to providing quality products and service
by working together to inspire creativity and to
enrich the lives we touch.*

Library of Congress Cataloging-in-Publication Data

Mead, Linda.
    The ABCs of making teddy bears / Linda Mead.
       p.   cm.
    ISBN 1-56477-332-9
    1. Soft toy making.   2. Teddy bears.   I. Title.
TT174.3.M38 2000
745.592'43—dc21

                                                      00-033934

# DEDICATION

―――――

*This book is dedicated to the memory of my father.*

*You fed my childhood imagination. You taught me that failure is just a step toward success.*

*You are with me every day.*

# ACKNOWLEDGMENTS

―――――

*To my mother—thank you for threading that first needle.*

*To my husband—thank you for your daily understanding, support, and encouragement.*

*To my daughters and grandchildren—thank you for life's joy.*

*All of you inspire my creations.*

# CONTENTS

# INTRODUCTION

WE BEAR MAKERS ARE ATTRACTED TO BEARS—NOT FOR THEIR PERFECT PROPORTIONS BUT FOR THE IMPERFECTIONS THAT REFLECT OUR OWN HUMANNESS. —LINDA MEAD

*E*VERYONE HAS A different answer to the question, "What is it about the look of a teddy bear that makes it special to you?" As a teacher, I've learned that the methods used to create a bear with personality are as individual and numerous as teddy bears are.

The fun and challenge of bear making is to create a bear unique to you—one whose personality talks to you. The challenge in writing this book has been to present a variety of appealing teddy bear designs and a range of construction methods that will help you create your ideal bear. The patterns include original designs from three Spare Bear Parts certified instructors: Sandy Sabo (VitoBear Company, Crystal Lake, Illinois); Linda Hartzig (What Else But Bears, Harrisburg, North Carolina); and JoAn Brown (Brown Bear Co., Blaine, Minnesota).

Whether you are a first-time bear maker, experienced enough to begin designing your own patterns, or somewhere in-between, this book was written for you. It is brimming with detailed information about tools, materials, special techniques, and instructions that are unique to teddy bear making.

The skill level required to make each bear is indicated by one, two, or three paw prints in the project directions, with three being the most difficult. Beginning bear makers should look for the pattern designs and instructions with a single paw print. An experienced bear maker will want to look for the patterns marked with two paw prints. These patterns offer unique design concepts and information, and some are easy-to-construct beginner patterns with added features to interest the experienced bear maker. Other patterns with two paw prints offer a construction challenge that requires the knowledge and experience of someone who has made many bears. All of these projects are well worth the time and effort because of their uniqueness and the valuable learning experiences that are gained.

Advanced bear makers will enjoy all the patterns in this book because they will broaden their knowledge of pattern design and artistry. Those patterns marked with three paw prints are especially important for developing pattern-making knowledge.

As an added point of interest, "Bear Facts" are sprinkled throughout the book and provide a little history of teddy bears as toys, as well as information about collecting them today. Helpful hints labeled "Artist's Tips" or "Artist's Reminders" are presented with each pattern. The reminders review instructions covered in the beginning of this book, and the tips cover the little things never found in patterns and seldom included in books. I've learned as a teacher that it can be the little things that turn your work from ho-hum to *zowie!*

# BEAR-MAKING TOOLS, SUPPLIES, AND MATERIALS

*T*HE TOOLS, SUPPLIES, and materials used in teddy bear making are on the following pages. If you are just beginning this hobby, I've included some suggestions for "make-do" tools, which include budget-minded alternatives. You may already have many of these tools in your sewing, craft, or household tool kits. These make-do suggestions are just that—tools to get you by to make your first or second bear. After making their first teddy bear, most people will tell you that it will not be their last. Bear making really is an addictive hobby! So much so that many people turn to selling their bears. As your activity in teddy bear making increases, you will want to replace the make-do tools with tools that are better in quality and ergonomics.

Before you begin a project, read through the pattern for the bear you are making and refer to the appropriate sections for assembly. This will give you an idea of what you'll need for your particular bear.

## NEEDLES

* Size 80/12 universal sewing machine needle for machine sewing.
* Small needles for hand sewing. Use the smallest needle that will do the job and that you can see to thread. The smaller your needle is, the smaller your stitches will be.
* Long, surgical-steel needles for attaching eyes. These needles stand up to the force required to penetrate a well-stuffed head. The triangle point penetrates the firm-pack stuffing. Use a needle at least 2" longer than the space between the eyeholes and the exit point. Use these needles for thread jointing as well. They are not, however, appropriate for thread sculpture.
* Doll needles for thread sculpture, which is a technique that uses thread and a long needle to add shape and dimension to an already stuffed toy. Do not use for installing eyes; doll needles bend too easily.
* Size 18 or 22 chenille needles for embroidering nose and mouth.

An assortment of needles and threads

## THREADS

IT IS NOT as important to match the thread color to the fur fabrics as it is with non-pile fabrics.

* High-quality, all-purpose cotton or cotton-polyester thread for machine sewing.
* Bonded nylon thread for hand sewing bears over 6".
* Waxed thread for attaching glass eyes. The wax helps hold the knot tight.
* Perle cotton for embroidering mouth and nose.
* Beeswax for coating perle cotton to create an antique look on an embroidered nose and mouth; also for coating all-purpose thread when hand sewing.
* Thread Heaven, a silicon coating that protects thread from wear. When applied to perle cotton, it helps the yarn slide through polyester stuffing without dragging strands of stuffing to the outside. Thread Heaven does not leave a visible coating on thread like beeswax.

## JOINTING TOOLS

REFER TO THE specific sections about bear joints for more detailed information on how these tools are used.

* Cotter key for bending cotter pins. It can also be used to curl single-wire eyes. Available in a variety of sizes. Look for T-style to support hand, which requires less strength to turn cotter pins. Make-do item: needle-nose pliers.
* Nut drivers, open-ended ratchets, or vice-grip locking wrench to tighten locknut and bolt joints. The bolt head and the locknut are different sizes. Be sure to purchase the correct size hardware to fit the nut and bolt you will be using. Make-do item: pliers.
* Small screwdriver to hold tap bolt while advancing the nut.
* Rivet tool to pinch the rivet on a rivet joint.

Types of jointing tools

# MISCELLANEOUS TOOLS AND SUPPLIES

Miscellaneous tools

✷ Awl to pull the fur free from the seams. Make-do item: a heavy-duty needle.

✷ Awl to create holes for eyes. Make-do item: the point of a pair of closed scissors.

✷ Felt-tip marker, ball point pen, crayon, or tailor's chalk to transfer the marks and dots from the patterns onto the fabric. Be sure that the marker you select is not water soluble and does not bleed through the fabric.

✷ Fray Check by Dritz, Aleene's Stop Fraying, or other seam sealant when making holes or to treat edges that fray or ravel.

✷ Forceps to turn small or difficult items right side out; also used to stuff small or hard-to-reach places. Forceps are available in a variety of sizes with straight and curved tips.

✷ Needle-nose pliers to curl cotter pins and single wire eyes; also used to grip needle when it is stuck. Use a rubber disk to grip needle; otherwise, pliers could damage the needle. Look for needle-nose pliers with a wire-cutter edge to cut wire on eyes.

✷ Pins to pin patterns to the fabric before cutting and to pin pieces together before sewing. Look for long pins with large, colored heads.

✷ Small, sharp, pointed scissors to cut the backing of fur fabric.

✷ All-purpose scissors for cutting patterns.

✷ Stuffing tool for stuffing bears. Look for a T-shaped tool that supports the hand. Make-do items: screwdriver, chopsticks, wooden-spoon handle, or unsharpened pencil.

✷ Tweezers to pluck fur from the muzzle.

✷ Wire brush to brush fur when grooming the bear. Available in various sizes to fit the bear. Make-do item: pet-grooming brush.

✷ Wrist-support gloves such as Handeze to help avoid carpal tunnel syndrome. Anyone involved in a craft or activity that uses a repetitive motion and places stress on the hands and wrists runs the risk of developing carpal tunnel syndrome. In addition to support gloves, use the proper tools for the job, hold the tools properly, take frequent breaks from repetitive or stressful activities, and alternate these activities with relaxing tasks.

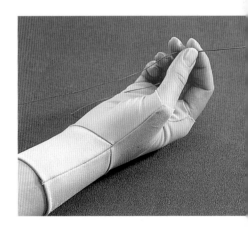

Wear a wrist-support glove.

# Fur Fabrics

The teddy bears presented in this book are made of mohair pile fabrics. Other possible fabric choices are synthetic knit-back pile and synthetic woven-back pile. Select the same pile height and density of fabric that the instructions suggest to ensure results that look most like the project photo. A longer pile will require more face trimming. Too long of a pile on a small bear may hide the shape of the body and limbs.

## Mohair Pile

Mohair is wool sheared from angora goats. Mohair pile fabrics come in a wide range of fur lengths, from very short to quite long, and fur density, from sparse to very dense. The pile can also be straight, wavy, or curly. The backing of mohair pile fabric is a coarsely woven cotton.

Mohair pile fabric was very popular for upholstered furniture and car interiors in the early 1900s, making it a natural choice for the early teddy bear manufacturers because it was the closest thing to real fur at that time. The pile height was limited to ⅛" to ¼" and had a very bristly feel. It was produced both in America and in Europe.

Today, the production of quality, teddy bear mohair fabric is limited to a few European specialty textile mills, even though the largest population of mohair goats is in Texas. In recent years these mills have broadened their line of teddy bear fabrics to include a large range of pile heights, colors, densities, and styles. Because of their price and limited use, teddy bear mohair pile fabrics are only available through mail order, at teddy bear shows, and at a few teddy bear shops and quilt fabric specialty shops. Refer to "Resources" on pages 152–153 for a list of companies that sell teddy bear products.

## Synthetic Knit-Back Pile

Synthetic knit-back pile fabrics are considerably lower in price than mohair pile fabrics and are available in local stores. They are thicker and generally denser than mohair pile fabric. Because they are synthetic, they are heat sensitive and are not dyeable. They can, however, be painted. See "Painting" on facing page.

Because the knit backing tends to stretch when stuffed firmly, the size of a bear made with this fabric versus one made with a woven-back fabric may be larger. This characteristic does not make knit-back fabrics good or bad. They just offer a different look and make these chubby bears quite lovable. However, if you select a pattern that has a large span of fabric without seams to control stretching, you may end up with a bear that loses its shape. This is most evident in the head, which will be stuffed firmly. You can control stretching by lining the head with a firmly woven fabric. You only need to line those pieces that will be hard or firmly stuffed.

To line a bear, lay the pile fabric wrong side up on a table. Place the lining fabric on top of the wrong side of the pile fabric, matching the two grain lines (see fig. 1). Place a few pins around the outer edges to hold the fabrics together. Pin the pattern piece to the fabrics, or draw around the pattern with a permanent marker. When cutting and sewing, treat the two fabric layers as one.

Mohair pile

Synthetic knit-back pile

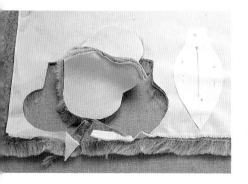

Fig. 1. Line knit-back fabrics to control stretching.

## Synthetic Woven-Back Pile

Synthetic woven-back fabrics, which stretch less than knit-back fabrics, are generally produced for luxury coat manufacturers. Like the synthetic knit-back pile, they are also heat sensitive and are not dyeable. Many of these fabrics are very suitable for collectible-quality teddy bears.

## Painting

Painting on mohair and synthetic pile fabrics allows you to truly personalize your teddy bear creation. Dye pens and permanent markers offer ways to highlight eyes, ears, and other features. Brushes and airbrush painting offer a way to paint larger areas of the bear for a unique design. More information about painting on pile fabrics is included with the instructions for making Missy the bear on page 00.

## Dyeing

Natural fibers like mohair are hollow and absorb color readily. Dyeing mohair pile fabric is so easy that once you try it you will wonder why you didn't try it sooner. You can create truly unique, one-of-a-kind bears by dyeing your own mohair pile fabric. The fabulous colors you can create will more than make up for the fussiness of the dyeing process.

Rit Dyes are easy to use and are readily available in most retail stores. To match a special color, you can write to the Rit Dye company and enclose a sample of the desired color. The address is on the package. They will advise you on which of their dyes to mix to achieve the desired color. Their liquid dyes create bright colors, while their powdered dyes are a better choice for that old-bear look. A tea bath after the fabric has dried will tone down the brightness of liquid dyes. Also, adding a very small amount of black, dark brown, or khaki dye to another color will help achieve an old look. Always test your color on a small swatch first before dyeing an entire piece of fabric.

You need not begin with white fabric. You can over-dye one fabric color with another dye. The color of your finished fabric will be determined by the combination of the two colors. Different fabric colors will not look the same, even when working with the same dye bath. Do a test swatch before dyeing the whole piece of pile fabric. Keep a record of the amounts of water and dye, water temperature, and length of time. No matter how carefully you follow your dyeing recipe, no two dye baths will produce exactly the same color. Be sure to dye enough fabric to complete your bear. Include the paw and foot pad fabrics in the dyeing process. Be sure to do a test swatch of the fabrics if they are different from the fabrics used in the rest of the bear.

If the fabric is a straight pile, dry the fabric in the dryer on a low setting. Hang curly and wavy fabrics on a hanger by the selvage or lay flat to dry. The heat of the dryer can relax the curl.

## REMOVING WRINKLES

Most mohair and synthetic pile fabrics are wrapped tightly on a roll at the mill. The fabric sometimes sits on the rolls for months, leaving sections of the pile badly crushed or with a distorted nap. See "Understanding Nap" on page 23. Just folding and shipping can create temporary wrinkles in more sensitive fabrics. Generally, there is nothing wrong with this wrinkled fabric. Given enough time, the wrinkles will relax and the nap will go back to normal. The best way to store pile fabrics is to hang them on clip-type pants hangers from the selvage edge and place them in a roomy closet.

If you have a wrinkled mohair pile fabric that you wish to use now, go ahead and make the bear. By the time you are done, most of the wrinkles will have relaxed. If the backing is so badly wrinkled that it will not lie flat to be cut, steam the fabric from the back side. You can use a hand-held steamer or the steam from an iron (see fig. 2). Be aware that brushing or applying water (hot or cold or steam) to string mohair will burst the strands, which will make them fluffy and stand up. The more heat and brushing, the fuller and fluffier it gets. This does not damage the mohair pile; it will just give you a different look.

Fig. 2. Left side of string mohair has been steamed.

Ironing synthetic pile fabrics can be risky. Too much heat, especially dry heat, can damage the fibers. A safer way to remove severe wrinkles is to place a wet bath towel in the dryer first to build up the humidity. After a few minutes, place the pile fabric in the dryer with the towel. Check every two to four minutes. Remove as soon as the wrinkles are gone.

There are two additional methods for removing wrinkles that do not involve heat, which makes them safer for mohair and synthetics. Spray the pile with water. Brush the pile in the correct nap direction. The nap of a pile fabric is the direction that the fur is manufactured to lie. Allow to air dry; then brush up the nap. You may also submerge the whole piece of pile fabric in water. Hand-squeeze the fabric, or spin the excess water out in your washer. Lay the pile fabric flat; then brush up the nap. Allow to air dry and brush the nap again.

## CLEANING

To keep your collectible teddy bears in good condition, display them in a dust-free environment, if possible. Keep lavender or cedar blocks near mohair bears to repel bugs. Do not use bug sprays on mohair. Vacuuming the bears occasionally will keep them fresh looking and dust free.

If you need to give a bear a bath, do not submerge a bear with hardboard disks, cardboard inserts in the foot pads, growlers, or other noisemakers. Use a clean sponge and a teddy bear-bath product or baby shampoo. The cleaning process is much like cleaning fine upholstery. Create lots of suds and use only the suds with an almost-dry sponge to gently clean the fur. Rinse the sponge frequently. To remove the suds, rinse with an almost-dry sponge. Brush the fur, allow the bear to air-dry, and brush up the nap. A hair dryer can be used to dry mohair.

# Paw Pads and Foot Pads

You may use a variety of materials for the paw pads and foot pads. Suede cloth is easy to sew and comes in a wide range of colors. Ultrasuede also comes in a wide range of bright colors and has the look of real suede. If you prefer real leather, use a thin leather so that the seam allowances will not be stiff and fight the curved edges. Recycled leather gloves are a great and inexpensive source for supple leather. Upholstery velvets and other fabrics sold for miniature teddy bears are also good sources for paw pads and foot pads. If you select a fabric that is thin and ravels easily, iron a lightweight interfacing to the wrong side of the fabric to stabilize it for sewing.

A piece of cardboard inserted in the foot will keep the foot pad from rounding or bulging when it is stuffed. Use cardboard from a shipping box or several layers of flat cardboard found on the back of a paper tablet. Cut the cardboard slightly smaller than the foot pad for a proper fit.

# Specialty Stuffings

There are a variety of stuffing materials available today, and each one serves a different purpose. I use the term "specialty" because most of them cannot be found in sewing stores. Only high-loft polyester and plastic pellets are available in most sewing stores. See "Resources" on pages 152–153 for places to purchase these specialty stuffings.

## Polyester

Polyester stuffings are the most popular stuffings because they do not mildew, cause very few allergies, meet fire safety standards, and are washable. These attributes make polyester stuffings the best choice for stuffed animals for children.

The high-loft version of polyester stuffing feels silky. The slick qualities of the stuffing allow the fibers to slip past each other, creating a non-packable, resilient stuffing that is great for soft-stuffed, huggable, and pillow-type bears. High-loft polyester stuffing will not pack hard enough to easily shape the head for a collectible-quality bear. It is a good choice to use in the body, alone, or with your choice of stuffings that add weight. High-loft polyester stuffing is available in most fabric and craft stores.

A firm, packable polyester stuffing is a good choice to hard-stuff and shape the head, as well as hard-pack the limbs and body of a collectible bear. The polyester fibers feel coarse, which makes them tangle and quickly pack hard and tight. This type of stuffing is more difficult to find in stores because it is rare to find it labeled as firm-pack or hard-pack stuffing. You may find suitable firm-pack stuffing sold as promotional goods or as a lower quality, high-loft stuffing.

Clockwise from left:
Firm-pack polyester, excelsior, kapok,
high-loft polyester, plastic pellets,
and glass pellets

## EXCELSIOR

Excelsior was the choice of the original teddy bear makers. Often mistaken for straw stuffing in old bears, excelsior is wood shavings—usually balsa wood. Either spaghetti or ribbon-style thin cut works the best for stuffing bears. Do not use dyed excelsior because the color may run when wet.

Excelsior is ideal for stuffing the muzzle because it is used damp. It dries hard and stands up very well to the pressure of embroidering the nose. You may stuff the entire bear with excelsior, or just the head or just the muzzle and use firm pack or kapok for the remainder of the head.

## KAPOK

This stuffing is a natural fiber from the kapok tree and is often mistaken for cotton in old bears. At one time kapok was the most popular product for stuffing, used for things like toys and furniture and World War II life vests. Its popularity has been replaced by a variety of polyester stuffings because polyester stuffings are non-allergenic and are cheaper to produce. Kapok packs hard, and because it has a silky texture, it fills more evenly and is less likely to have gaps and soft spots than polyester.

## STUFFINGS FOR WEIGHT

Copper shot, plastic, and glass pellets are good choices of stuffing that are used to add weight. The amount used is dependent on the amount of weight you wish to add to the bear. Add kapok or polyester high-loft stuffing to finish filling the cavity. Used alone these pellets create a beanbag type feel. Copper shot is the heaviest of these three and can be purchased at most gun shops. Plastic pellets are the lightest of these three and are available at sewing and craft stores. Glass pellets have rounded edges and are only available through teddy bear specialty suppliers.

## SAFE STUFFING CHOICES

All the above products are safe and acceptable stuffing products when used as instructed. There are only four states—Ohio, Maine, Pennsylvania, and Massachusetts—that enforce stuffing laws, which are also known as bedding laws. Artist bears are often exempt from these laws because of the low quantities produced by an artist or because the end user is intended to be an adult. Over the years, in an effort to reduce stuffing costs and add weight, a few bear makers have used products that are hazardous or simply will not last the life of a collectible-quality bear. Dried peas, beans, rice, and coffee beans will all attract bugs and rodents, as well as be subject to damage from moisture. Kitty litter can cause breathing problems, and it can also be treated with chemicals that could be damaging to mohair. Sand and aquarium gravel are acceptable choices if they have been sterilized by baking. Chemicals used in sterilizing can leave a residue that can harm mohair. The use of lead shot has given a few artists lead poisoning.

If you buy artist bears, be sure to ask the artist what stuffing materials were used. This is for your own safety as well as for the life of your investment.

# EYES

Types of eyes

EYES FOR TEDDY bears are available in many different forms, sizes, and colors. Early teddy bear manufacturers used leather shoe buttons, and sometimes larger boot buttons, for eyes. Some teddy bear makers still like to use shoe buttons. Authentic vintage shoe buttons are difficult to find. Glass eyes replaced the shoe buttons in teddy bears and are widely used today. They are available with and without pupils. Some glass eyes have a wire loop on the back, while others are on a single wire with an eye at each end. A recent addition on the market is reproduction shoe buttons made of frosted glass.

Plastic safety eyes are essential when making teddy bears for children. They also come in a wide range of sizes and colors.

Onyx beads are a good choice for miniature and small teddy bears. They are available in 2 mm, 3 mm, and 4 mm.

Glass eyes and onyx beads are installed after the head is stuffed. Plastic safety eyes must be installed before stuffing the head.

# NOSES, MOUTHS, AND CLAWS

NOSES, MOUTHS, AND claws are usually embroidered with perle cotton. Sizes 3 and 5 are used on medium to large bears. Size 8 perle cotton is used for smaller bears, and embroidery floss is used on miniatures.

Some bear makers prefer to make noses from leather, suede, or velvet. Plastic safety noses are a good choice for children's bears and need to be installed before stuffing the head.

# JOINTS

THREAD JOINTING WAS one of the first ways that toy makers jointed early teddy bears. Today this method, which involves attaching the head and limbs with thread, is used for miniatures and smaller bears. It is also a fun way to loosely joint a reproduction bear.

Because thread jointing did not hold up well for children's toys, a method using connected rods that extended into the bear limbs was devised. This was used for only a short time because the rods wore through the fabric. Circles of heavy cardboard were then used and held together by a turned nail similar to today's cotter pin. Later some manufacturers used a type of rivet.

Today's joint disks are available in hardboard so that they will stand up to years of handling without bending. They are made in a variety of sizes, from ⅜" to 3½" in diameter. Since these disks are made of wood, they are not submersible in water.

Plastic joints are also widely available for use in teddy bears made for children. They are washable and durable. They also come in a variety of sizes and are easy to install in knit-back fur fabrics.

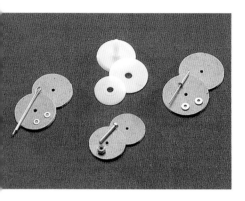

Types of joints

Hardboard disks are held together with one of several methods: cotter pins, locknuts and bolts, or rivets. The location of the opening for turning the bear part right side out and stuffing will determine the type of hardware you use to joint the bear.

Read through the directions for the bear you are making to find the type of joint system used. Detailed instructions for assembling the different jointing systems are described in "Jointing" starting on page 44.

# BEAR-MAKING TECHNIQUES

## GETTING STARTED

### PREPARING THE PATTERN

Select a pattern appropriate to your skill level. In order to make the bear look as it was intended, accuracy is very important in cutting the pattern and the fabric. Make a photocopy of the original pattern or trace it. Adhere craft-weight, iron-on interfacing to the backs of the pattern pieces to make the paper pattern stronger so that it will hold up to repeated pinning. If you prefer to trace the pattern onto the fabric, you will need a thicker pattern. Paste the copies of the pattern pieces onto thin cardboard. Always cut the pattern out on the *inside* edge of the line.

Because most bear patterns are used over and over again, the edges will eventually wear down from cutting and tracing. This could alter the shape of the pattern. After making three or four bears, check the pattern against the original and make a new pattern if necessary. For a more durable pattern, trace the pattern onto plastic template material with a permanent marker.

All the pattern pieces for the bears in this book are full size except for Circus Bear. The pattern pieces for Circus Bear have been reduced so that the bear could be included in the book. To make the full-size version of this pattern, you will need to enlarge the pattern pieces by 170 percent on a copy machine. See "About the Pattern" on page 143 for details on how to do this.

You will need to make a pattern for each piece. For left and right pieces (mirror images) such as arms, you have two options. You can cut one pattern piece and label both sides with the appropriate marks. Then when you cut the pieces from fabric, cut one first, turn the pattern over, and cut the second one. Or you can consider making two pattern pieces—one for the left and one for the right. To do this, trace the pattern onto a piece of paper. Place a second piece of paper under the traced pattern and cut both layers at once, remembering to cut on the inside edge of the lines. Transfer the pattern markings to the front of each left and right piece.

Seam allowances are already included in all the pattern pieces so that you do not need to add seam allowances when cutting out the fabric pieces. Make a note of the size of the seam allowance on each pattern piece. Generally it will be ¼"; however, some patterns may have areas with a different seam allowance. Use an awl to make tiny holes in the pattern at the dots indicated for the joints. Make small clips, about ⅛" long, at match lines along the seam edge. You can also transfer the match lines to the back of the fabric with a permanent marking pen.

## UNDERSTANDING GRAIN LINE

An experienced sewer understands the importance of straight of grain and of how a bias seam line effects any fabric project. Because many people come to bear making without basic sewing knowledge, the importance of straight of grain and bias are often overlooked. Some published patterns do not even mention the straight of grain and instruct the reader to follow the apparent nap direction of the fabric when cutting.

To understand why cutting the fabric by following the nap direction could be a problem, you have to know that fabric is made of threads (called yarns) that are woven together at right angles. This gives fabric the ability to stretch or remain stable, depending on the grain line you cut along. The vertical yarns, or weft, of the lengthwise grain run parallel to the selvage edge or factory-finished edge of the fabric and have little or no give, while the horizontal yarns, or warp, of the crosswise grain run from selvage to selvage and usually have some give. Lines drawn at angles to the straight grain lines are considered bias. A true bias runs at a 45° angle to the lengthwise and crosswise gains and has the most stretch. If the nap is lying in the direction of the grain line, you'll have no problems constructing your bear. Unfortunately, the nap tends to shift on fur fabrics when they are shipped and stored. Following the direction of the nap instead of the straight of grain can lead to sewing disasters. For example, arms and legs cut on the bias will twist to one side, or the face cut on the bias will stretch as it is stuffed. It may not be a lot, but it will be noticeable. Another example that almost everyone can relate to is a twisted leg on a pair of jeans. No matter what you do—iron it, starch it, or wash it—that leg does not hang straight. This is caused when the two pieces of a leg are cut on different grain directions.

Attempting to sew together two teddy bear limb pieces along mismatched grain lines can cause sewing problems, too. The bias does not have a thread to hold it stable. Consequently, long edges cut on the bias are subject to stretching as they are handled and sewn. The bias edge is bound to stretch, while the piece cut on the straight of grain will be stable. The sewing machine or the thickness of the fur is often blamed for mismatched edges and stretched and wavy seams. Cutting on the bias, however, is the biggest culprit for these problems. Taking care to cut the fabric out on the straight grain as marked on the pattern is the beginning of a quality project. All of the projects in this book include straight of grain arrows.

On mohair pile fabric, the selvage edge is the plain weave without the mohair. On knit-back fur fabrics, the selvage edge is thicker and different from the rest of the fabric (see fig. 3). Do not use this selvage edge when cutting out your bear. Also, knit fabrics have no stretch on the lengthwise grain but do stretch on the crosswise grain. See "Synthetic Knit-Back Pile" on page 14 for how to line knit-back fabric. The backing of knit fabrics also has an easy-to-follow vertical ridge for the straight of grain. On woven fabrics, both the lengthwise and crosswise grains are stable and do not stretch.

Fig 3. Selvage of woven-back mohair (left) does not have fur; synthetic knit-back fabric (right) shows fur extending beyond the selvage

## UNDERSTANDING NAP

The direction in which the fur feels smooth and lies straight is called "with the nap." The fur will feel rough "against the nap." Identifying the nap direction on straight pile fabrics is easy. Finding the manufactured nap direction on distressed and curly fabrics is much more difficult. To identify the manufactured nap direction, look at the cut edge from the wrong side. You will see fur showing beyond the cut edge in the direction of the nap. With a felt-tip marker or crayon, mark the direction of the nap with an arrow along the selvage edge. This will give you an easy reference for nap direction as you lay out your pattern pieces. Remember to also follow the grain line of the fabric when laying out the pattern pieces.

It is very important that you plan the nap direction on your bear. Mismatched nap directions are very obvious on a finished bear. The patterns in this book are marked for the nap and grain direction. Generally, the nap should lie in a downward direction. However, on sparse furs you will get a fuller look if the direction of the nap is up. This is also true if the nap is turned forward toward the face. Fur brushed against the nap will also appear fuller and denser.

On mohair piles, the fur fibers may get pushed in a different direction during shipping and storage. When you lay the pattern on the fabric, point the arrows toward the cut edge. After the bear is made, you can steam and brush the nap to correct the direction with a clothing steamer or a steam iron (see fig. 4). Set the iron for maximum steam and hold it a few inches away from the mohair. Repeat the brushing and steaming until the nap is lying in the correct direction.

For extremely stubborn areas on mohair, you may need to wet the area with water from a spray bottle. You can even use the iron to press it in place. Do not, however, use any products such as hair spray or gels. Over time, these kinds of products will collect dust. Water and heat work the best. Also, do not use steam on synthetic pile fabrics. Use cool water and a brush to control unruly synthetic fur.

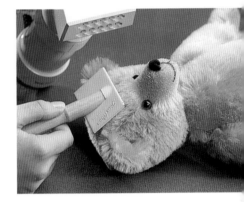

Fig. 4. Steam and brush the fur to correct the nap.

## LAYING OUT THE PATTERN

Several of the bear patterns include a pattern layout diagram indicating how pattern pieces should be cut from the fabric. Following these diagrams will assure that you will be able to cut all the pieces from the required amount of fabric. If the pattern does not include a pattern layout diagram, plan the layout of all the pattern pieces before you cut so that you can determine the most efficient use of the fabric. Start with the largest pieces; then fill in with the smaller pieces.

Lay a single layer of fabric on a table with the wrong side facing up. Be sure the fabric does not drape over the edge of the table or it may distort the cut pieces.

To match the grain line indicated on the pattern to the straight grain on the fabric, fold the pattern piece along the printed grain line and line up the folded edge with the fabric grain (see fig. 5). Remember to pay attention to the nap direction also. Unfold the pattern and secure it with long pins.

If you made durable cardboard or plastic patterns, trace around the patterns onto the fabric back with a felt-tip marker on light fabrics and tailor's chalk on dark fabrics. Before you cut, check that all the pieces are following the grain and the nap arrows. If you need to change the layout, use a different color marker for the second

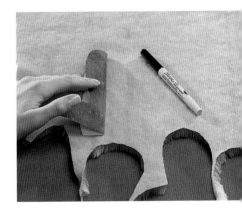

Fig. 5. Align grain line on pattern to fabric grain.

plan. Remember to cut away the marker line so that you do not distort the pattern size and shape.

## CUTTING THE FUR FABRIC

Small, sharp, pointed scissors work best. To cut the fur fabric, slide the lower blade along the backing and cut only the backing—never the fur. Make small cuts to maintain control. For easy reference, keep each pattern piece with its corresponding fabric piece.

## TRANSFERRING THE PATTERN MARKINGS

Transfer all matching marks, and eye and ear placement marks, to the wrong side of the fur fabric piece by using a felt-tip marker, ball-point pen, crayon, or tailor's chalk. Be sure the marker you select is not water soluble and does not bleed through the fabric. If you prefer, you can make clips into the seam allowance to indicate matching marks.

### Tailor Tacks

Use tailor tacks to transfer marks for eye and ear placements to the front of the fabric (see fig. 6 ). Tailor tacks are thread tails used to mark the ear, eye, and mouth placements on the right side of the fabric. They can be attached before the pieces are sewn together or after the pieces are sewn but before stuffing.

To make a tailor tack, thread a needle with a contrasting color of thread or use thin yarn for large bears. Take a small stitch from the fur side at the placement mark indicated on the wrong side, leaving a long tail of loose thread. Tie the two thread ends together so they don't come out as you are stuffing and working on the bear.

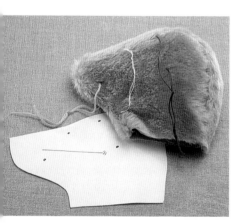

Fig. 6. Use tailor tacks to transfer marks for eye and ear placements.

# SEWING BASICS

A BEGINNER SEWER will be able to sew most of the bear pieces without any problems. Simply align the match marks on the patterns. Backstitch at the beginning and end of each seam, and remember to leave an opening for turning and stuffing where marked on the pattern. You can sew the entire bear by hand, by machine, or a combination of both. Always read the instructions carefully before beginning the project.

## MACHINE SEWING

Fur fabrics produce a great deal of lint. Clean your sewing machine often when working with fur fabrics and keep it in good working order. Use a straight-stitch throat plate for more control when sewing narrow seam allowances. Set your machine for straight stitch, about 12 to 14 stitches per inch. Thread your sewing machine with a high-quality, all-purpose thread. Do not use nylon or heavy-duty thread for sewing bears on your machine. Use a size 80/12 universal needle, which is designed for both knit and woven fabrics.

Practice sewing with pieces of scrap fur fabric to be sure the tension settings on your machine are correct. To test the tension, thread the top and bobbin with different colored threads. If the tension is set properly, the stitch line should only show one color of thread on each side of the pieces. Refer to your sewing-machine instruction book to adjust the tension if needed.

The seam allowance on most of the bear patterns in this book is ¼". The smaller bears, however, are made with a ⅛" seam allowance. Additionally, some patterns use a combination of ¼" and ⅛" seam allowances. Be sure to read the directions to make sure you are using the correct seam allowances when sewing the bear parts.

Most sewing machines do not have a ¼" seam allowance mark. To assure accurate sewing, place a piece of tape along the throat plate of your machine at the ¼" mark to guide the cut edge of your fabric. If you build up multiple layers of the tape, you can use the edge of the tape as guide to keep the fabric from slipping and causing a wider seam. When you have made the necessary adjustments to your sewing machine, you are ready to begin sewing your bear.

Pin two layers of fabric right sides together, matching all marks. Tuck the fur toward the right side as you pin. Place the pins perpendicular to the seam line. After pinning, lay the bear part or limb on a flat surface. If it lies flat, you are ready to sew. If the part twists or an edge turns up, this means that the grain lines are not matched. Unpin the area and shift the pieces to realign the edges until the part lies flat (see fig. 7).

On longer furs, sew a small basting-size stitch, which is 7–8 stitches to the inch. After the first row of basting stitches, it is important to groom the seams. This is an important step to making the seams look neat on the right side. To groom, open the seam allowance and use an awl or a heavy needle to lift the fur caught along the stitch line and pull the fur free (see fig. 8). When the inside is done, use the awl or heavy needle to groom the outside of the seams.

Sew a second row of smaller stitches over the first row. This process will assure tight seams that will hold up to firmly packed stuffing and prevent unsightly ridges of fur from sticking through the seam line. This is especially important on straight pile furs and if you plan to trim the muzzle. If, after trimming, you find that you missed pulling some of the fur out of the seams, pluck the fur with tweezers. A second method often recommended to prevent fur from sticking in the seam allowance is to trim the fur from the seam allowance before you sew. You need to be very accurate though, and cut only the fur within the seam allowance.

If you are having trouble fitting the two layers of fur under the presser foot, or if the top layer of fur pushes ahead and causes the end of your seam to be uneven, there are two reasons for this. First, all fabrics shift to some degree when sewn on a sewing machine. The feed dogs move the bottom fabric back while the pressure from the presser foot prevents the top fabric from moving through the machine at the same rate. The bulk of fur fabric makes this a noticeable problem. A walking foot is available for most machines (see "Resources" on pages 152–153) and may help with this problem. It moves the top layer through the machine at the same rate as the bottom layer. If possible, try it on fur fabrics before you buy. On some machines a walking foot reduces the much-needed space under the foot.

The second reason is that under pressure, the fibers of the fur—especially soft silky furs—work against each other or "walk," and add to the shifting. To help avoid this, reduce the pressure from the presser foot if this is possible on your machine.

Fig 7. The example on the left shows an edge that is turned up, which indicates that the grain lines are not matched.

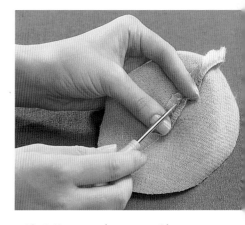

Fig 8. To groom the seams with an awl, pull up the fur caught in the stitching line.

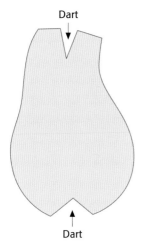

Dart

Dart

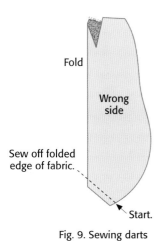

Fold

Wrong side

Sew off folded edge of fabric.

Start.

Fig. 9. Sewing darts

Pinning the two fabric layers carefully also helps keep them aligned, especially if you pin across the stitch line; you can sew right to the pin before removing it. Holding the fabric both in front and behind the foot without pulling also helps.

The patterns for some of the bears include one or more darts. Darts help remove fullness from the outer edge of a bear part and distribute this fullness to the area around the point of the dart. To sew a dart, fold the body piece with right sides together and align the inside edges of the dart so that the ends of the dart meet. Following the seam allowance recommended for the bear you are making, start stitching at the outside edge of the piece and stitch toward the point of the dart. Maintain the same seam allowance width as you sew along the edge of the dart and off the edge of the fabric (see fig. 9).

### Sewing Small Bears

For the tiniest of teddies you can use the sewing machine to sew those pieces that are mirror images (arms, legs, and ears) and do not have darts. Before cutting the fabric, select the pattern pieces to be sewn by machine. Make a copy of the arm, leg, or ear pattern pieces, but cut them out on the stitch line. Be sure to write on the patterns "without seam allowance" so that you do not confuse them later with a pattern that includes the seam allowance.

Select a piece of fabric twice the size of the pattern pieces, allowing at least ¾" around the pattern plus enough space to fold the fabric in half along the grain. Lay the pattern without the seam allowance on the fabric, following the nap and grain line, and trace around the pattern. With right sides together, fold the fabric in half along the grain line. Pin the folded edge and around the outer corners of the fabric. Stitch on the drawn line, running the machine slow enough that you are able to follow the small curves exactly. Leave an opening if it is marked on the pattern. Carefully trim away the excess fabric, leaving the size seam allowance noted in the original pattern (see fig. 10).

### Pivoting

When you see the term "pivot," it means you will turn a corner while sewing a seam. To sew these seams, pin up to the pivot mark. Sew to the pivot mark, but do not remove the fabric from the machine. Instead, lower the needle into the mark; then raise the presser foot. Pivot the fabric on the needle in the middle of the seam. Notice that the edges of the pieces will not line up past the corner where you just pivoted. Re-align the remaining edges of the pieces so that they match, lower the presser foot, and continue sewing.

### Easing to Fit

The term "easing" is used wherever one side of a seam is slightly longer than the other. It means that you will need to adjust, or ease, the extra fullness of the longer piece by slightly stretching the short piece as you pin it to the longer piece. You distribute the fullness evenly along the seam line. Then you sew the seam with the longer piece facing up so that you can judge how even the fullness is. Sewing this way will also allow you to catch and correct any puckers before they happen.

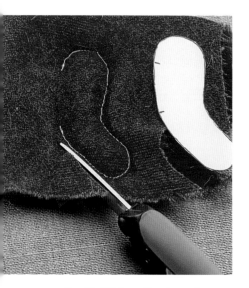

Fig. 10. Stitch on the drawn line, and trim away excess fabric.

# Hand Sewing

For hand sewing teddy bears, select the smallest needle that will do the job and that you can see to thread. The smaller the needle, the smaller the stitches you can make. Small, tight stitches make tight seams, which is important for any bear that will be hard stuffed. As you sew, tug on the thread to snug up the stitches. It is all right to have the seam line slightly gathered. This is contrary to what you have learned about sewing on thinner non-pile fabrics. When the bear is stuffed hard, the seam will stretch slightly and smooth out the gathered stitches.

The thread you select depends on the fabric and size of the bear. It is more important to match the thread to non-pile fabrics than to fur fabrics. The thread will not show on fur fabrics if the stitching is done tightly. Bonded nylon thread is strong and works very well to hand sew bears over 6", but it is too heavy to use on smaller bears. For bears smaller than 6", use all-purpose sewing thread coated with beeswax to prevent wear as the thread repeatedly passes through the fabric. You can also use Thread Heaven to coat the thread.

### Double Running Stitch

On longer furs, use two rows of running stitches. For the first row, take small stitches by running the needle in and out of the fabric in a straight line, maintaining the correct-width seam allowance. Groom the seam from the wrong side by pulling the fur caught in the stitch line. See page 25 on grooming seams. For the second row, stitch in the same line as the first row but insert and exit the needle between each of the previous stitches.

### Backstitch

A backstitch is good to use on very short furs where the seams do not need to be groomed. Make a full stitch forward (⅛") and a half stitch back (¹/₁₆"), keeping the correct-width seam allowance.

### Overcast Stitch

Use an overcast stitch to sew together the raw edges of the ears and to sew the ears to the head. Do not use this stitch to sew the bear parts together. It does not result in a tight, close-stitched seam, and it prevents access to grooming the seams from the wrong side.

### Closing Stitches

See "Ladder Stitch" on page 51 on how to close the stuffing opening. See "Spider Web Stitch" on page 52 on how to close the neck on the head after stuffing.

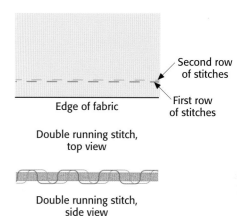

Second row of stitches

First row of stitches

Edge of fabric

Double running stitch, top view

Double running stitch, side view

Backstitch

Overcast stitch

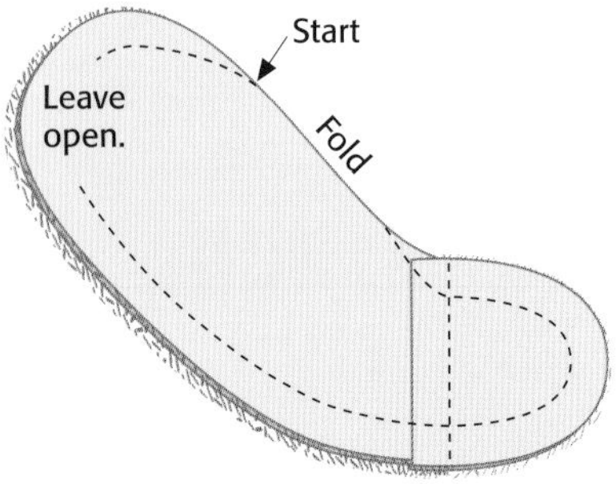

Fig. 11. Gradually sew off fold
at wrist edge.

# SEWING CHALLENGES

## ONE PIECE ARMS

When sewing an arm where the inside and outside arm are one piece, some beginners are not sure how to end the seam at the wrist where the fold begins. Fold the arm along the fold line with right sides together, match marks, and pin. Starting at the top of the arm on the fold, sew around the arm until you reach the paw pad/wrist seam. At this point, gradually begin narrowing the seam allowance until you sew off the fold (see fig. 11). Don't forget to leave an opening if one is marked on the pattern.

## FOOT PADS

Foot pads are challenging because you are sewing straight edges on the leg to curved edges on the foot pad. You can use the sewing machine to sew foot pads on larger bears. On smaller bears, however, you will find it much easier to sew the foot pads by hand. Whichever method you use, the following steps will help you sew them easily without any folds or puckers.

1. Sew the leg seam(s) first. With right sides together and the foot pad on top, pin the toe and heel marks to the corresponding seams or marks on the leg. Keep the pins inside the seam allowance as much as possible and perpendicular to the seam line. If the pins extend much beyond the seam line or point in the direction of the seam, you may be creating more puckers.

2. Place a pin halfway between the first two pins on each side of the foot. Pin again at ¼ the distance, keeping the fullness evenly distributed. Remember to keep the foot pad on top and flat (see fig. 12). It may help to pull the edges of the foot opening out to meet the foot pad. If you still have trouble making the edges fit, make small clips in the seam allowance of the foot pad or the edges of the foot opening as needed.

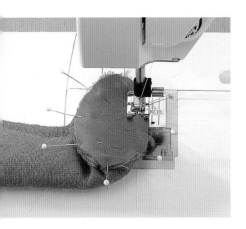

Fig. 12. Foot pad pinned

3. With the foot pad on top, start sewing at the toe and continue all around the foot pad to the point where you started (see fig. 13). Be sure your seam allowance is exactly the size required by the pattern. Any wider or narrower will cause puckers along the seam line.

4. Examine both sides after you complete the seam, looking for folds or puckers. If you find any, cut the thread, smooth out the area, and repin. Then sew again.

## HEAD GUSSET

There are four pattern designs and sewing methods for the nose area of the gusset: triangle, box corner, square, and rounded. To assure that the fabric doesn't shift, which can cause a crooked muzzle, sew the seams with the gusset face up. Pinning evenly is not enough to compensate for the fur fabric shifting or "walking" as you sew the muzzle. You can sew from the nose to the back or from the back to the nose. The choice is yours, but both gusset seams must be sewn with the gusset piece face up. This means that the first seam you sew will have the bulk of the fabric

Fig. 13. Foot pad being sewn
by machine

to the left of the needle, as usual. For the other side of the gusset, the bulk of the fabric will be to the right of the needle. Use the left side of the presser foot as your seam gauge. This might seem a little strange at first, but it will definitely keep the muzzle straight. Before you start sewing the second seam, check the left side of the presser foot to be sure it measures ¼" from the needle. If it doesn't, shift the needle position or mark the throat plate with the proper seam allowance. Leave an opening in the head or neck as marked on the pattern.

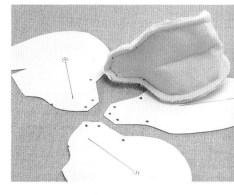

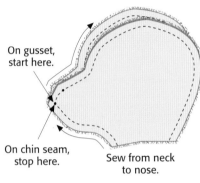

Triangle muzzle

### Triangle Muzzle

The triangle is the easiest muzzle to sew. It offers a clear area, without a seam, that makes it easier to embroider a nose.

1.  Match the marks on the head gusset to the marks on the side head pieces and pin. Sew each side from the nose to the end of the gusset. Finish the seam from the gusset to the neck edge as the pattern requires (see fig. 14).

2.  Sew the chin seam from the neck to the nose, backstitching at the nose (see fig. 14). When stuffing, mold the nose area so that the triangle remains vertical. Don't let it become flat and even with the top of the muzzle, or the muzzle will be too pointed.

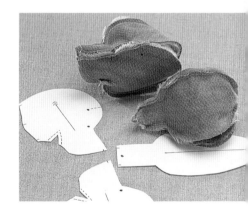

On gusset, start here.

On chin seam, stop here.

Sew from neck to nose.

Fig. 14

### Box-Corner Muzzle

The box-corner muzzle is easy to sew but takes some thought.

1.  Match the marks on the head gusset to the marks on the side head pieces and pin. Sew each side from the corner of the nose to the end of the gusset. Finish the seam from the gusset to the neck edge as the pattern requires (see fig. 15).

2.  Fold the muzzle in half and open the seam allowances at the nose corners. Sew from the fold, down the chin seam, and to the neck (see fig. 16).

3.  Refold the muzzle so that the chin seam is lined up with the center of the head gusset. The nose area now forms a triangle. Stitch across the base of the triangle between gusset seams to form the width of the muzzle. Trim away the point of the triangle (see fig. 17).

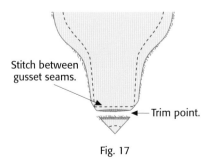

Box-corner muzzle

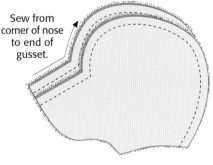

Sew from corner of nose to end of gusset.

Fig. 15

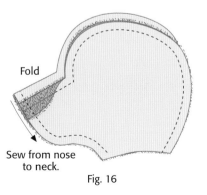

Fold

Sew from nose to neck.

Fig. 16

Stitch between gusset seams.

Trim point.

Fig. 17

BEAR-MAKING TECHNIQUES • 29

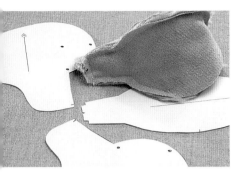

Square muzzle

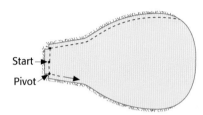

Start

Pivot

Fig. 18. For second side, start sewing at center of nose and pivot at corner.

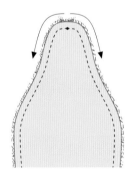

Rounded muzzle

Fig. 19. Sew from nose to back of gusset.

## Square Muzzle

The square muzzle takes a little effort to keep even, but it forms a nice, wide nose. Cut the seam allowance out of the corners of the muzzle as indicated on the pattern.

1. Pin and sew the chin seam from the nose to the neck.

2. With the chin seam allowance open, match and pin the seam to the center of the gusset. With the gusset on top, sew across the nose from one cut-out corner to the next cut-out corner, stopping with the needle down at the corner. Pivot the fabric on the needle. Align the edges of the gusset with the side head piece and sew to the back of the gusset.

3. To sew the second side, do not begin sewing at the corner. With the gusset again on top, begin sewing at the center of the gusset/chin seam. Sew to the cut-out corner and stop with the needle down. Pivot at the corner and sew to the back of the gusset. Finish the seam from the gusset to the neck edge if necessary (see fig. 18).

## Rounded Muzzle

The rounded muzzle is the traditional style used in the older teddy bear designs from bear makers like the famous German teddy bear company, Steiff. It is the most difficult to sew well by machine. A beginner may have better success sewing the rounded muzzle by hand.

1. Pin and sew the chin seam from the nose to the neck.

2. With the chin seam allowance open, match and pin the seam to the center of the gusset. Clip into the seam allowance of the side head pieces and pin them to the gusset, easing the pieces as necessary. With the gusset on top, sew from the nose to the back of the gusset (see fig. 19).

   Repeat for the other side, with the gusset still on top. Finish the seam from the gusset to the neck if necessary.

# Turning Pieces to Right Side

Turn pieces right side out after sewing is complete and marks have been transferred to the right side. Forceps are handy to turn small parts or narrow limbs to the right side. With the forceps, grasp the seam allowance furthest from the opening. Gently push the forceps toward the opening so that the fabric slides over the forceps smoothly (see fig. 20).

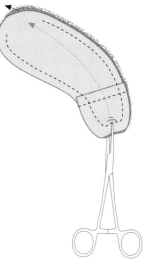

Fig. 20. Turn piece to right side.

# ASSEMBLING THE BEAR

*T*HE HEAD STUFFING and shaping information is presented next because, after sewing all the parts, most new bear makers are anxious to complete their bear's head. However, the various methods used to joint teddy bears determine the sequence of jointing and stuffing. This is because some hardware requires access to both sides of the joint to tighten them, while other types of jointing hardware require stuffing the bear first and then tightening from only one side. Because no one method is right for everyone or for every bear pattern, this book includes several hardware choices and options for the opening placements. See "Jointing" starting on page 44 and "Turning, Stuffing, and Joint Openings" starting on page 50. Read all the pattern and jointing directions carefully to make sure you are assembling your bear in the correct order. Once you have experienced using several jointing methods, you may use the jointing hardware of your choice to assemble the bear in any order you wish.

## CREATING THE HEAD SHAPE

THERE IS MUCH more to the art of creating a wonderful teddy bear face than placing eyes and doing neat nose stitches. The shape of the head frames the eyes, nose, and mouth. And, together with the position and size of the ears, the head shape gives an impression of the human qualities of age, gender, personality, and even mood. The pattern may determine the size of the head, but it is the art of the stuffing process that dictates the very important shape of the head and face. This hands-on interaction with pliable materials offers such a wide potential of subtle differences and yes, imperfection, that no two bears can be identical. The fascinating aspect of bear making is what the face will turn out to be—this time. Even when using the same pattern, the variety of faces can be endless. Little differences in how you hold the head as you stuff can lengthen or shorten the muzzle, resulting in a quick change from a blue ribbon to a pink one! That change in muzzle length will often require a change in the eye and/or the ear locations and sometimes the size of the nose, too. The little-boy look you achieved with your first use of a pattern may turn into a sweet old lady as you complete your second bear with the same pattern!

The length of the muzzle is only one attribute that defines gender and age. A large forehead, full cheeks, and large eyes can be feminine or very childlike. A short forehead is often related to an older male. These are just a few of the many combinations used to achieve various looks. To understand what features represent

## MECHANICS OF STUFFING A HEAD

To HELP YOU understand the mechanics of stuffing a head and how you can control the stuffing process to achieve the look you planned, try the following exercise. Begin by selecting a favorite pattern and cut, sew, and mark two heads from the same fabric. Use tailor tacks to transfer the pattern markings to the right side of the fur. Use excelsior, firm-pack polyester, kapok, or any combination of stuffing you prefer. Refer to "Using Specialty Stuffings" below to learn how to achieve a firm, stable shape to the head.

**Head #1:** As you stuff the first head, pay close attention to how you naturally hold the bear as you work. That comfortable, natural position is how you achieve your bear's look by "accident." Once you are conscious of how you hold your work as you stuff, your future work can be more consistent to that original "happy accident." Add the ears and eyes as marked on the pattern.

Compare the finished bear head with the pattern photo. Identify the differences in head shape. Is the head you made taller or shorter, thinner or fatter? Is the muzzle longer or shorter? If you put the eyes and ears in the locations marked on the pattern but the face doesn't look the same as the photo, it is because of the way you held and shaped the head as you stuffed. If you are happy with the first head, great. Remember how you achieved the shape so you can repeat it the next time. To learn how you can change the shape of the head, continue with the exercise.

**Head #2:** As you stuff the second bear head, study the photo as you stuff. Now change the natural way you hold and stuff the head to achieve the shape that you see. Work the head like clay to mold the shape of the face. The change will probably feel strange to your hands. It takes some effort to make changes to things we naturally do. Can you see and feel how much control you have in shaping the head? Everyone stuffs and shapes teddy bear heads differently. The goal is to learn what you do so that you can consciously repeat it or avoid it the next time you make a teddy bear.

what attribute, study the drawings that accompany children's books. This art is very simple yet can convey gender, mood, and more through facial characteristics. Another source to study is antique family photos. It is fascinating to see the differences and similarities in facial features in different generations of a large family. These exercises will make you more aware of the face shape and size in relation to eyes, ears, nose, and mouth.

Teddy bear making is a very personal art form. To achieve just the right combination of head and face shape, with features in just the right size and position, is the artistry that produces a bear that "speaks to you." Whether by conscious design or happy accident, it's the personal touch each artist brings to each individual bear that gives it personality, charm, and appeal.

## USING SPECIALTY STUFFINGS
### Hard Stuffing

To give a long life to the head and face shape of a collectible-quality teddy bear, the head should be hard stuffed. Use excelsior, polyester firm-pack, kapok, or a combination of these to achieve it. When using a hard, "packable" stuffing, use very small pieces in the small areas. Excelsior should be lightly misted with a spray of water to make it packable. A walnut-size amount, or two rounded tablespoons before it is crushed, is a good starter. Flattening the stuffing piece into a small, thick pancake also works well. As the area begins to fill, use a stuffing tool to add stuffing around the outside edges between the previous stuffing and the fabric wall. As the area you are stuffing increases in size, you may increase the amount of stuffing accordingly. Remember to mold the head shape as you stuff, similar to molding clay. Excelsior is ideal for stuffing the muzzle because it dries hard and stands up to the pressure of embroidering the nose. Continue with excelsior, or finish stuffing the head with kapok or firm-pack polyester until it is very firm like a grapefruit, which will allow the eyes to set deep into the fur when installed. To close the stuffing openings, see "Ladder Stitch" on page 51.

### Soft Stuffing

High-loft polyester stuffing is best used by taking a handful about the size of a small apple and pulling on it to increase the size. Continue pulling on the handful in different areas until it is about double the original size. Place this in the cavity to be stuffed. Repeat until the cavity is full but still huggable. Do not use high-loft polyester stuffing in the head because it will not pack hard enough to maintain a stable head shape over the life of the bear. To close the stuffing openings, see "Ladder Stitch" on page 51.

### Weighted Stuffings

Copper or steel shot, plastic, and glass pellets are good choices of stuffing if you want to add weight. Totally filling the body and limbs will create a beanbag type feel. You can also use smaller amounts for a portion of the bear and then add kapok or polyester high-loft stuffing to finish filling the cavity. You can put weighted stuffings in a separate bag, but it is not necessary. Because of their weight, they will stay in the lowest point and not migrate above the other stuffing. To create a firm pack, shake the shot or pellets to settle them and then add more until the cavity is filled. To prevent the shape of the weighted stuffing from dimpling paw or foot pads, stitch a layer of polyester fleece to the inside of the paw or foot pad prior to assembling the bear. To close the stuffing openings, see "Ladder Stitch" on page 51.

# EYES

**Supplies:**
Awl to make holes in fabric
Long surgical needles
Needle-nose pliers
Rubber disk to grip needle
Waxed thread

THE EYES AND nose are the focal point of the bear's face and reflect the bear's personality. The eyes and nose form a triangle I call the "personality triangle." The personality triangle is framed (just like a picture) by the "ears and mouth triangle."

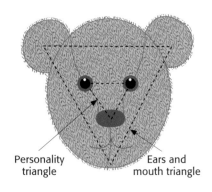

Personality triangle        Ears and mouth triangle

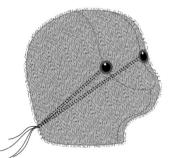

Fig. 21. Threads pulled to back of neck

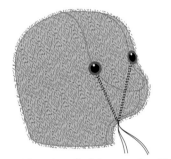

Fig. 22. Threads pulled down under chin

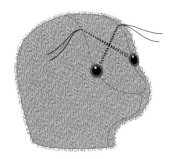

Fig. 23. Threads pulled to opposite sides

Fig. 24. Roll the wire down into an oval shape.

Both triangles work together to create the bear's personality. The size, shape, and placement of each facial feature affect the size, shape, and placement of all the other facial features.

If you choose to move the eyes from the original pattern placement, consider the placement of the other features by pinning the ears and a temporary felt nose in place. Eyes look best when they are kept close to the seam where the muzzle turns into the forehead. Remember when selecting the eye position that eyes are better too low than too high and better too close together than too far apart. *Also, if you want a trimmed muzzle, plan and trim the area before installing the eyes because it will help determine the placement of the eyes.* If you want to trim the fur where the eyes will be placed, you need to do this before installing the eyes. Plastic safety eyes for children's bears need to be inserted before the head is stuffed, while all other eyes can be inserted afterward.

A product called Try Eyes is a handy way to determine the size and placement of eyes. Try Eyes are glass eyes with pins attached and come in different sizes so that you can experiment and move the eyes to a location you like. Be sure to measure from the tailor tack to the new placement for both eyes to make sure that the eyes are placed evenly on the head.

Refer to children's storybook art to see how the size and placement of eyes and ears portray different personalities and emotions. Use these ideas to create new looks for your bears.

Finally, when placing eyes, keep in mind that the shape of the forehead is affected by the exit location of the eye threads.

❋ Knotting the threads to the back of the neck, just above the neck joint (see fig. 21), creates a high forehead like Sasha's on pages 74–79.

❋ For eyes set low on the muzzle, like those for the bear Billi on pages 68–73, you will pull the eye threads under the chin (see fig. 22).

❋ Forming an X under the nose bridge by tying the threads at the opposite side ear placement will raise the bridge (see fig. 23), much like Old World Bear on pages 62–67.

## GLASS EYES

If you are using prelooped glass eyes, skip to the section on page 37 regarding attaching thread to the eye.

*To prepare glass eyes on a single wire, cut the wire about 1½" from the eyes with the wire-cutter edge on pliers.*

1. With needle-nose pliers, roll down the wire a little less than ½" from the cut end. The wire should look like a fish hook (see fig. 24).

2. Move the pliers to the back side of the hook and roll down the wire again. You now have an oval shape.

3. Roll the oval shape down one more time so that the cut end of the wire is facing the back of the glass eye. It is very important that the cut end not point out, or it will catch on the fabric and stuffing as you insert the eye into the head.

*To attach thread to eyes:*

Cut a piece of waxed thread twice as long as the thickness of the head plus 18". Secure the thread to the wire loop on the back of the eye (see fig. 25).

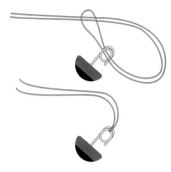

Fig. 25. Secure thread to the eye loop.

*To install eyes with threads that tie at the back of the head or under the chin:*

1. Use an awl or the closed point of small scissors to make holes at the eye marks. Work the tool around to form a pocket in the stuffing to fit the eye loop.

2. Thread both cut ends into the needle. Do not knot the end.

3. Insert the needle into the eyehole. If the eye loops won't go into the eyehole, gently reshape the wire for a better fit.

4. Exit both threads at the back of the neck or under the chin (see thread exit as described in "Eyes" introduction on pages 35–36 and figure 26).

5. Remove the needle and leave the two eye threads to be tied later.

6. Repeat for other eye.

7. Pull the two sets of eye threads so that the eyes set deep into the fur. Tie the ends in a secure knot and bury the ends.

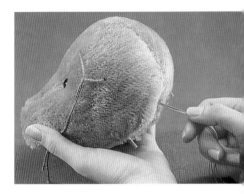

Fig. 26. Eye installation with exit at back of neck

*To install eyes with threads that tie in separate locations:*

1. Tie a separate piece of thread to eye loop.

2. Thread only one of the two strands from eye onto the needle. Insert the needle into the eyehole and exit at the ear placement (see fig. 27).

3. Repeat for other strand of thread, exiting right next to the first. Tie the two threads together, pulling tightly to indent the eyes.

4. Repeat for other eye, exiting at other ear.

## Eyelids

Use a nonravel fabric such as upholstery velvet or Ultrasuede to make eyelids for your bear.

1. Cut a small rectangle as wide as the eye and slightly longer than the width of the eye. Experiment with different sizes for the look you want.

2. Fold the fabric in half lengthwise. Trim each end at a 45° angle. When open, the piece will have a V cutout at each end, like the ends of a piece of ribbon. Poke a small hole for the eye loop close to the edge on one long side (see fig. 28).

3. With wrong sides together, hand sew the folded V edges together with bonded nylon thread. Leave the thread tail to sew the eyelids to the face after the eyes are secure.

4. Slip the eye loop into the hole in the eyelid and attach the eye thread (see fig. 29). Run threads through the head, and pull threads tight to indent eyes; knot securely. Bury the thread tails.

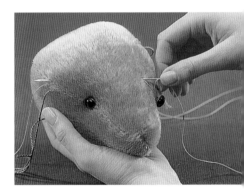

Fig. 27. Eye installation with exit at separate locations; green yarn tailor tack indicates ear placement.

Fig. 28. Eyelid piece with cut ends and hole for eye loop

Fig. 29. Eyelid with eye in place and ends sewn

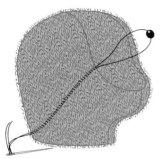

Fig. 30. Exit at back of head.

## Onyx Bead Eyes

Black onyx beads are available in sizes 2 mm, 3 mm, and 4 mm. They are a good choice for miniature and small teddy bears.

Follow these steps when tying threads together to secure bead eyes:

1.  Thread the bead onto black bonded nylon thread. Thread both ends of the thread into the needle.

2.  Insert the needle at the eye mark and exit at the back of the head (see fig. 30).

3.  Repeat for the other eye and exit right next to the first set of threads.

4.  Pull the threads tight to indent the eyes; knot the threads from each eye together. Bury the thread tails.

## Plastic Eyes

Plastic safety eyes come in two pieces: the eye and the safety washer. Plastic, cup-shaped Life-Lyk eye backs are also available for safety eyes but are sold separately (see fig. 31). The purpose of the eye back is to push the fabric up around the safety eye to make the eye look more like it is inset into an eye socket. Safety eyes are very easy to install and are done before stuffing.

1.  From the wrong side, cut a tiny hole in the fabric at the eye mark.

2.  From the right side, place the stem of the eye through the fabric hole. Place the Life-Lyk eye back on the eye stem. The eye should set inside the cup of the Life-Lyk eye back, with the edges of the Life-Lyk eye back pushing the fabric up around the eye.

3.  Place the safety washer onto the stem. The washer will only go onto the stem one way. This prevents the washer from working off by itself.

I have had a very stretchy, knit-back fabric stretch so much that a small, plastic safety eye without a Life-Lyk eye back came out of the hole in the fabric. The washer was still attached to the eye stem. To prevent this, put a small drop of fabric glue on the eye mark. Allow the glue to dry before you cut the hole for the eye. Should you create a stretched eyehole or cut a hole in the wrong place, mend it with a few stitches on the wrong side of the fabric. The fur on the right side of the fabric will hide the stitches. If you are not sure how secure your mending is, add a little fabric glue to the stitches on the wrong side.

Fig. 31. Life-Lyk back in place before washer (left); safety eye and washer (right).

## Thread Sculpture

**Supplies:**
Bonded nylon thread
Long doll needles

THIS IS A technique that uses thread and a long needle to add shape and dimension to an already stuffed toy. However, the longer the fur, the less these modifications will show. Thread sculpture is often used to correct uneven eyes and ears (see fig. 32). You can take stitches between the eyes to bring them closer together and raise the bridge of the nose. Or, take stitches from the eyes to the ears to raise the eyes and create a brow. Just remember that the location and tightness of the stitches that you do on one side must be repeated for the other side; otherwise, your bear will be lopsided. I recommend that you only do one stitch at a time and repeat it on the other side before you continue with the first side.

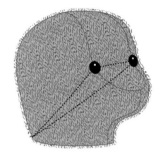

Fig. 32. Using thread sculpture to correct uneven eyes

Select a doll needle that is longer than the distance to be spanned. Be sure that the needle you select has an eye large enough to hold the bonded nylon thread.

1. Cut 1 piece of thread 48" long. Fold the thread in half and thread both cut ends into the needle, but do not knot the ends.

2. Take a tiny stitch in an inconspicuous place like the neck; then pass the needle through the loop end of the thread and pull tight to secure (see fig. 33).

3. Remove one thread from the needle and proceed with stitching. Use second thread to stitch the other side. You can hide the sculpture stitches by taking very small stitches, by using a matching color of thread, and by not catching the fur in the stitches. Knot securely and bury the ends.

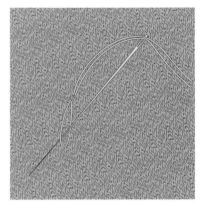

Fig. 33. Pass the needle through the loop end of the thread.

Sometimes the stuffing is packed so hard that you will need to take several stitches in the same place, pulling each stitch as tight as possible to attain the desired look. Once you master molding as you stuff, you will probably not need to do as much thread sculpture since you can achieve most of the look you want by molding the head as you stuff.

# TRIMMING THE MUZZLE FUR

**Supplies:**
Small scissors
Tweezers
Wire brush
Electric trimmers (optional)

TRIMMING THE MUZZLE is another way to create a variety of different looks. You can choose to trim a little or a lot, depending on the look you are after. Before you start to trim the muzzle on your bear, practice trimming on a scrap piece of fabric first. If you use very small, sharp-pointed scissors to trim the fur, you will have more control as you cut.

Lay the scissors flat to the fabric and take tiny cuts. Use a wire brush against the nap to raise the nap and make it easier to trim. Trim around the muzzle first, establishing a cutting line or length to cut the fur on the rest of the muzzle. Then work against the nap to trim away the remaining fur. Look at the face from different angles to judge if the remaining length is even and there are no ridges. Take your time when trimming, and remember—it doesn't grow back!

Fig. 34. Remove stubble with tweezers.

Electric trimmers also work great for trimming the muzzle. Be sure to practice on a scrap piece of fabric first.

If you like the fabric backing to show without the fur stubble, trim the fur as close as you can to the backing. Then use tweezers to pluck the remaining stubble from the fabric (see fig. 34).

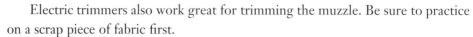

# Nose and Mouth

**Supplies:**
Perle cotton
Size 18 or 22 chenille needle

**Optional**
Beeswax
Clear fingernail polish or varnish
Thread Heaven

### Perle Cotton Stitched Nose

If you can do an embroidery satin stitch, you will have no problem doing a neatly stitched nose. Stitching the nose is a simple process but takes a bit of practice to do it well. For best results, beginners should make small noses with a minimum amount of stitching. As you gain experience, you can increase the size and complexity of the nose.

I recommend that you do the bear's nose first before stitching the mouth because you need to know where the bottom of the nose will be before you can do the mouth. The first step in making a good stitched nose is to sew the muzzle and chin seams with perfect seam allowances. It is impossible to center a stitched nose if the chin seam line isn't centered. The second step is having a hard-packed, stuffed muzzle. It is surprising how much pressure is exerted on the nose while stitching it. Excelsior makes the best muzzle stuffing because it dries hard when packed damp.

The size of perle cotton to use depends on the size of the bear. You can use size 5 (thin) or size 3 (thicker) for most medium and large bears. I prefer a combination of size 5 for the nose and size 3 for the mouth. For small and miniature bears, use size 5 or size 8 perle cotton.

The early bear makers did not have a hard-finish perle cotton as we do today. Instead, they would wax yarn to make it sturdy enough not to wear as the nose was stitched. Today's perle cotton does not need to be waxed to add strength. However, if you want the look of the old bears, you can wax the perle cotton by passing it over beeswax. Additional wax may be added after the nose is stitched by rubbing the beeswax on the nose. Hold the bear's nose near a light bulb or other heat source to melt the wax into the yarn. Repeat as necessary to achieve the desired look.

Thread Heaven will help the perle cotton slide through the stuffing. Unlike beeswax, it does not leave a visible coating on the perle cotton.

An easy way to ensure an evenly stitched nose is to make a felt pattern or

Fig. 35. Stitch nose over a felt pattern.

purchase a pre-cut felt pattern called Nose Templates (see fig. 35). The commercial nose patterns are self adhesive. If you make your felt pattern, you will need to lightly glue it in place and allow it to dry before stitching. Before you can glue the nose to the bear, however, cut the felt nose slightly smaller than the desired shape of the finished nose. Where the nose will be stitched, trim the fur to the backing. You will be stitching over the felt, not through it. The felt adds padding that increases the size of the nose. To make a very large, bulbous nose, add more layers of felt.

If you are not using a felt pattern, trim the fur and remove the stubble with tweezers to prevent little strands of fur from sticking up between the stitches.

An alternate method to using a felt pattern is to draw the nose shape on the fabric. Trim the fur before drawing. Use a permanent marker the same color as the perle cotton to draw the outline of the nose; you can even color in the space with the marker. Be sure your stitches cover the outline.

The point at which you need to insert the needle to anchor the perle cotton depends on the type of nose you are making. If you are starting with a felt pattern, make a small knot in the perle cotton and take a small stitch under the felt to hide the knot. If you do not have a felt pattern, slide the needle between the stitches along the chin seam. Exit at the top center of the nose. Pull the thread until the knot slips between the stitches in the chin seam (see fig. 36). If the knot will not slip between the stitches, the needle may have caught a strand of fabric. Remove the thread and try again, making sure that the needle goes between the stitches and does not catch the fabric.

To end your stitching, take the last stitch at the corner of the nose and slide the needle into the fabric under the nose a couple of times. Cut the perle cotton at the surface.

If you like the look of a shiny nose, use clear fingernail polish or varnish on the perle cotton after the nose is stitched. See painted Missy starting on page 80. The first few coats will soak in and not show. Continue adding thin coats, allowing the polish to dry between each coat.

### Triangle Nose

The triangle shape is the easiest nose to stitch because you only have one edge to keep straight. After anchoring the perle cotton (under the felt or through the chin seam), exit at the center top of the nose. Insert the needle at the bottom point of the triangle each time. Exit on alternate sides of the first stitch to fan the stitches out across the top of the nose, keeping the stitches right next to each other. Continue with stitches on alternate sides to make the desired size nose (see fig. 37). Take care to keep the top edge of the nose straight and even.

If you wish, you can add a second layer of stitches on top of the first. Run the second layer in the opposite direction from the first layer, starting at the top of the triangle and tapering down to the point (see fig. 38).

### Rectangle or Square Nose

Stitching a rectangular or square nose is a little more difficult than a triangle nose because you have two edges to keep even. The rectangle or square nose is stitched the same as the triangle nose, starting at the center top and alternating

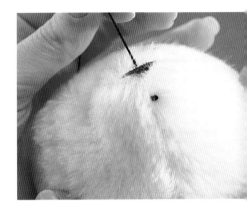

Fig. 36. Pull knot between chin seam stitches.

Fig. 37.
Triangle nose

Fig. 38.
Optional stitching

Fig. 39. Rectangle nose

Fig. 40. Embroidered nose with nostrils

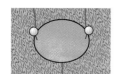

Fig. 41. Pin oval between two muzzle seams.

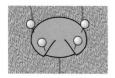

Fig. 42. Fold pinched sides down to form nostrils.

Add stuffing.

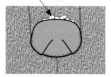

Fig. 43. Stitch bottom and sides with overcast stitch.

Fig. 44. Take small stitch in nostril area.

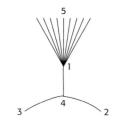

Fig. 45. Steps for embroidering the mouth

stitches from side to side (see fig. 39). For more interest, you can add longer stitches on each side of the nose or in the center (see fig. 40).

## FABRIC OR LEATHER NOSE

You can use any fabric that does not ravel to create a fabric nose. Ultrasuede, suede cloth, and upholstery velvet are good choices. Noses made from ovals are easy to do.

1. Cut an oval from fabric in desired size. Pin it between the two muzzle seams (see fig. 41).

2. Pinch two sides of the oval and bring them forward to form nostrils, leaving some fabric between the nostrils. Place pins to hold the indentations for nostrils (see fig. 42).

3. Starting on one side, use an overcast stitch down one side, across the bottom, and up the other side of nose. Add a small amount of stuffing at the opening along the top (see fig. 43).

4. Run the needle underneath the nose fabric from muzzle seam; then take a small stitch in nostril area (see fig. 44). Return needle to muzzle seam. Pull stitch tight, repeat stitching, and add stuffing as needed until desired shape is achieved. Repeat for other nostril; then sew top of nose area.

## MOUTH

**Supplies:**
Perle cotton
Size 18 or 22 chenille needle
    (Be sure the needle is long
        enough to reach through the chin.)

**Optional**
Thread Heaven

Follow these steps to embroider the mouth, referring to the numbered diagram at left (see fig. 45).

1. If you use the same perle cotton for the mouth as you do for the nose, exit at the bottom center of the nose (1), which should be at the chin seam. If you use another color, thread a single strand of perle cotton on a long needle and knot the end. Insert the needle through the chin seam as described in "Perle Cotton Stitched Nose" on page 41. Exit at the bottom center of the nose (1).

2. Insert the needle (2) and push the needle through the chin and out (3). Do not pull thread too tight; allow the thread to drape between points 1 and 2.

3. Now place your needle under and then over the draped thread in preparation for the next stitch (4). Run the point of the needle along the chin seam to

decide where you want point 4 to be. As you move the needle down along the seam, the center line between the two sides of the mouth will become longer. As you lower the position of point 4, you will see a smile starting to form with the draped thread. Insert the needle when you find the right amount of smile or pout for the expression you are after. Exit at the bottom center of the nose.

4. Adjust the tension on the thread to set the mouth. If you pull too tight, the thread may get buried in the fur, in which case you may not see part of the mouth. If you leave the thread too loose, it may shift and the mouth will not hold its shape. When you are satisfied with the shape of the mouth, knot the thread securely and bury the thread tail under the nose.

By experimenting with the placement of points 2, 3, and 4, you will find that you can create many different expressions. I like to make points 2 and 3 wide apart, with 4 lower than 2 and 3. If the thread is slightly loose, this creates a nice smile. If necessary, tack the thread along the curve of the smile to keep it in place.

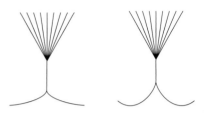

You can create many different expressions.

# EARS

**Supplies:**
Bonded nylon thread
Long chenille needle

Traditionally, teddy bear ears are cupped or stitched to the head in a C shape. In the older Steiff bears, the ears were always placed following the gusset seam along the head for about one quarter of the ear length before they curved down and around and lined up with the eye.

You can achieve a variety of personalities by simply changing the location of the ears. Some patterns have ear placement marks indicating where I placed the ears on the head, and other patterns leave the placement to your imagination. Feel free to experiment with ear placement and the curve of the ears. For example, you can make your bear Pooh-like by taking a tuck in the middle of the ears and sewing them on the high area of the gusset seam (see fig. 46).

Try pinning the ears in different places on the head. Once you decide on the right placement for the ears, look carefully at the bear to see if both ears are straight and even. Look at the ears from the front, back, side, upside down, or even in a mirror.

To add interest to the bear's face, make the front half of the ear from a short, light color fur or from the same color as the rest of the bear but in a different fabric like felt.

To make ears, pin the pattern pieces together with right sides facing. Sew along the curved edges, leaving the straight edges open. Be sure to use the proper seam allowance as instructed in the pattern. Turn the ears right side out.

Use tailor tacks to transfer ear placement marks from the wrong side to the right side of the fabric. If your bear does not have ear placement marks, experiment with a variety of placements as described above.

Fig. 46. Fold a pleat in the center of the ear.

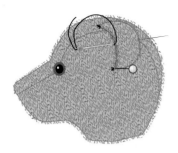

Fig. 47. Stitch ear at three points;
then add more stitches as needed.

1. Sew the straight edge of the ears together with bonded nylon thread, a long needle, and an overcast stitch.

2. With the thread still attached to the ear, insert the needle in the head at the first tailor tack; pull tight. Take several stitches in the corner of the ear to secure it. Position the other corner of the ear at the second tailor tack and hold it in place with a long pin. Slide the needle under the fur, through the head, to the other ear corner and secure it with several stitches. The ear should curve. Now slide the needle under the head fabric to the middle of the ear and stitch it in place (see fig. 47).

3. The ear is now attached at three points. For miniatures and smaller bears, this may be all that is needed. For larger bears, add more stitches between the three points to attach the ear securely. Tie off and bury the knots.

# JOINTING

THE METHOD USED to joint a bear determines how and when to stuff the limbs and head. Some hardware only requires access to one side to be tightened. This allows you to stuff and close each piece before jointing it to the body. This is definitely an advantage on big bears. Some people like this jointing method so well that they use it on all bear sizes. Cotter pins, glued locknuts and bolts, and tap bolts can all be used for this method because they only require access to one side when tightening.

There are two jointing methods that require access to both sides of the hardware to tighten: rivets, and locknuts with an unglued bolt. This means you can joint all of the limbs and the head to the body before you stuff. When working on small to medium-size bears, this is not a problem and is sometimes even preferred. The larger the bear, the harder it becomes to stuff with everything attached.

There are also a number of choices of where to leave the stuffing opening. You will learn in "Joint Placement: Neck" on facing page how it works to your advantage to sew the neck closed to place the joint and stuff through a gusset seam.

If you are a beginner, you may find the number of choices you have in how and when to joint or stuff to be a little confusing. Once you have experienced each method by making the various patterns in this book, you will be able to select the best method or combination of methods that work for you.

## JOINT PLACEMENT: LIMBS

By changing the placement of the joints, you can affect the pose and personality of the bear. Attaching the legs in front of the side seams will cause the toes to turn slightly in when standing. Attaching the legs behind the seams will cause the toes to turn out. Attaching the arms behind the side seams will opens the arms (ready for a hug). Attaching the arms in front of the side seams will turn the paws in slightly, creating a shy, reserved appearance.

## JOINT PLACEMENT: NECK

Changing the neck joint placement will make major changes in your bear's personality. Sew the neck edge closed as an extension of the chin seam, and leave an opening in one of the gusset seams for stuffing and jointing. Then you can make a hole in the head/neck seam for the joint according to where you want to position the head. For example, if you want the muzzle tilted upward, make the hole in the head/neck seam just behind the neck center. If you want the muzzle facing down toward the tummy, place the hole just in front of the neck center. Insert the assembled joint, stuff the head, and close the opening.

The opening along one of the gusset seams is also used if you need to tighten the joint hardware from both the body and the head. This is necessary when using rivets or locknut and unglued bolt joints.

As with the head/neck joint, changing the body joint placement will impact your bear's personality. To do this, the seam at the top of the body must be sewn closed. Placing the joint in front of the shoulder seam will tilt the head forward; behind the shoulder seam will tilt the head upward. To create a side tilt, place the joint hole to one side of the front seam.

My favorite head and neck placement is to insert the joint hardware behind the center on the head/neck seam (chin will tilt up) and in front of the shoulder seam on the body (head will lean forward; see fig. 48). Experiment with different placements on the same pattern to see how changing the tilt of the head affects the personality of your bear.

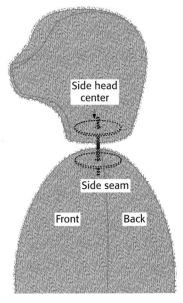

Fig. 48. Joint placement for chin tilted up and head forward

## HARDBOARD JOINTS

There are three important points to remember when jointing a bear:

⋆ Always pass the joint hardware through a hole in the fabric. Either cut or force a very small hole with an awl. Do not cut seam stitching. If the joint is to be attached right at a seam, skip stitches in the seam line to accommodate the hardware.

⋆ Always assemble the joint from the limb direction into the body so that the bulk of the joint is inside the body. Be sure that the fabric is not wrinkled between the disks or the joints won't be tight.

⋆ Double check that you have all the necessary washers in the right place. Missing washers means the hardware will pull through the disk holes.

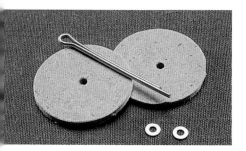

Cotter-pin hardware

## *Cotter-Pin Joints*

**Supplies:**
Awl to make holes in fur fabric
Cotter key or needle-nose pliers
Hardboard disks
Steel cotter pins
Steel washers

Cotter pins are probably the most widely used for teddy bear joints because they are inexpensive, require no glue, and can be tightened with a common pair of household needle-nose pliers. They can be attached to the body before or after you stuff and close the head and limbs of your bear. Sometimes it is difficult to get really tight joints, but using a cotter key makes tightening much easier.

There are two different types of cotter pins: those with a rounded eye and those with a T-shaped end. In cotter pins made of soft metal, the rounded eye of the pin may be pulled through the washer if the bear maker is really strong. To solve this problem, place a washer on a single leg of the cotter pin (instead of on both legs) and move it up to the eye. This additional washer on the single leg cannot be pulled through the washer next to the hardboard disk. Another solution is to use T-shaped cotter pins. The ends of these pins cannot be pulled through the washer. T-shaped cotter pins are also a good choice on small bears because the joint is flatter; you won't feel the bump of a cotter-pin eye in very small limbs.

### Assembly

The following diagram illustrates the order of assembly for a cotter-pin joint. The washers are on the outside of the disks with the limb and body fabrics between.

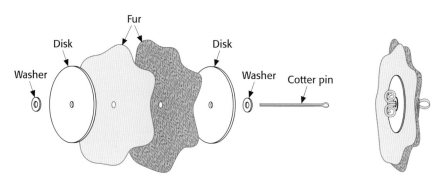

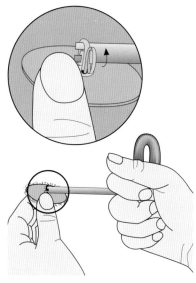

Fig. 49. Curl cotter-pin leg away from you.

1. Assemble the cotter-pin joints and insert them in the appropriate body parts.

2. Slip the slot of a cotter key onto the longest cotter-pin leg and curl it down and away from you. You can also use needle-nose pliers. The motion is similar to opening a sardine can. As you work, pull up on the cotter pin. This will help make a tighter joint. Keep the curl large and do not allow

the curl to "spiral" out to the side or you will not be able to tighten the joint (see fig. 49).

3.  Turn the cotter pin so that you can curl the second cotter-pin leg in the same manner, away from you. Adjust both legs of the cotter pin to assure equal pressure on the joint disk.

**Jiggle Joints**

A very wobbly joint can be created by using two rounded-eye cotter pins, eye to eye. Use smaller cotter pins than you normally would use for the size disks required for the bear.

1.  Place one leg of a cotter pin inside the eye of a second cotter pin. Place a washer, a disk, and a second washer on one cotter pin and curl tight with a cotter key.

2.  Put the joint in position by inserting the straight cotter-pin legs inside the limb, out the joint hole, and into the body. Add a washer, the disk, and the second washer (see fig. 50).

3.  Curl the second cotter-pin legs tight. The joint is secure but the limbs jiggle and give the bear a lifelike feel once the bear is stuffed.

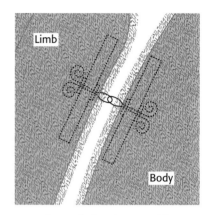

Fig. 50. Jiggle-Joint assembly

### *Locknut and Bolt (or Tap-Bolt) Joints*

**Supplies:**
Awl to make holes in fur fabric
Hardboard disks
Locknuts, and bolts or tap bolts
Two nut drivers or wrenches
Two-part epoxy glue (optional)

To use locknut and bolt joints, you will need access to both sides of the joint. This jointing method should be used with bear pieces that are unstuffed. A locknut has a nylon washer inside of it that prevents the nut from backing off the bolt. However, you may unscrew the nut with a nut driver.

If you apply a two-part epoxy glue (for wood and metal) to glue the bolt to the hardboard disk, you can tighten the nut from only one side. Be sure to get some glue onto the bolt threads that are in the disk hole and under the head of the bolt. Allow plenty of time for the glue to dry before attempting to complete the joint.

A tap bolt is similar to a regular bolt, but it has a slot in the end opposite the head. This slot allows you to hold the tap bolt still with a small screwdriver while advancing the nut with a wrench to tighten it from one side. The head or limb can be closed before being attached to the body. Another advantage is that you don't need to use any glue.

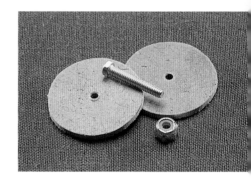

Locknut and bolt joint

Washers are not necessary for locknut and bolt or tap-bolt joints, provided that the head of the bolt will not fit through the disk hole.

## Assembly

### Locknut and Unglued Bolt

The following diagram illustrates the order of assembly for a locknut and bolt joint, and tap bolt.

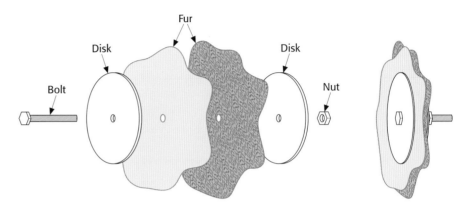

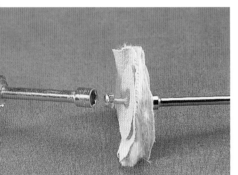

Fig 51. Use nut drivers for both sides.

1. Put the bolt into the disk hole and advance it all the way until the head of the bolt is against the disk. Place the assembled unit through the hole in the limb and body and onto another disk.

2. Attach the nut with the nylon washer facing out. To tighten, hold the bolt head with one nut driver while twisting the nut onto the bolt with a second nut driver (see fig. 51). Before stuffing, the joint should be so tight that it will hardly move. After stuffing, the fabric will stretch and reduce the bulk between the disks and this may loosen the joints. Adjust all the joints to the same tightness.

### Locknut and Glued Bolt or Tap Bolt

1. Place the assembled glued bolt or tap bolt through the hole in the limb. Complete the stuffing and close the opening.

2. Place the bolt into the body joint hole and another disk. Tighten the locknut on glued bolt with one nut driver. Tighten the locknut on the tap bolt with a wrench while preventing the tap bolt from turning by holding it still with a screwdriver (see fig. 52).

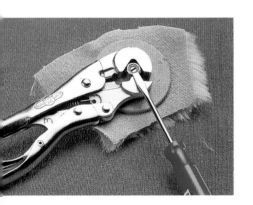

Fig 52. Hold tap bolt still with a screwdriver.

## *Rivet Joints*

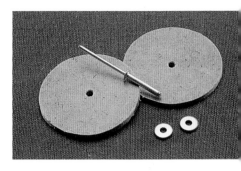

Rivet joints

**Supplies:**
Aluminum rivets
Aluminum rivet washers
Awl to make holes in fur fabric
Hardboard disks
Rivet tool

A rivet type of joint was used in bears and other toys as early as the 1920s. The advantage to using rivet joints is that they do not loosen with age and use. With a little practice, you can do a number of joints in a very short time. Rivets are a popular jointing method with teddy bear artists who need to produce a large quantity of bears. You must install rivet joints before stuffing the bear.

The best rivets to use are aluminum with a ⅛" diameter by ¾" grip range. I recommend aluminum because it is a soft metal, which is easier to stretch and break. A rivet has a thin end, which is called the stem, with a sleeve over it. The washers are also aluminum. To avoid corrosion, it is recommended that you use the same metals together.

You will also need a rivet tool. Please review the directions on the back of the rivet tool package before using it. Most rivet tools come with two "nose pieces." The one installed is for ⁵/₃₂" diameter rivets. The second one, for ⅛" rivets, is attached lower on the handle. Use the small tool that comes with the rivet tool to change the nose piece to the ⅛" size.

The ⅛"-diameter rivet fits well into the joint disks. The ¾" grip range is a special long size not sold in most stores (see "Resources" on pages 152–153). If you are using a very dense fur and ¾" is not long enough, you may need to trim the dense furs from between the disks, or use a cotter pin or locknut and bolt for the joints.

### Assembly

1. Place the stem end of the rivet into the tool nose piece. Open the handles as wide as possible to allow the rivet to "set," or fall in place. The stem will be all the way into the tool and the sleeve will fit against the nose piece.

2. Place the jointing pieces onto the sleeve end of the rivet in this order: washer, disk, limb fabric, body fabric (fur side to fur side), disk, and washer (see fig. 53).

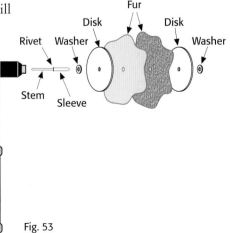

Fig. 53

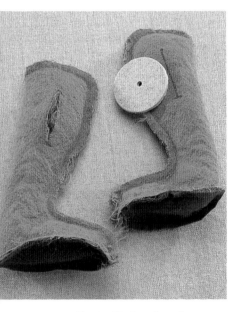

Fig. 54. Mark and cut the slash openings.

3. Squeeze the handle of the rivet tool to force the rivet downward and crush the sleeve. This stretches and breaks the stem off. If it does not break the first time you close the handles, open the handles and move the rivet stem further into the nose piece and squeeze the handles again. Repeat until the stem breaks.

4. Remove the stem end from the rivet tool by opening the handles as wide as possible and turning it upside down. The stem will fall out.

## TURNING, STUFFING, AND JOINT OPENINGS

This section describes the three types of openings and the various jointing systems used on the bears in this book. I recommend that you try the different jointing systems to see firsthand which one you like the best. If you prefer to use a different opening location than the one specified in the pattern, you may do so. Remember that you may need to change the jointing hardware and the stuffing sequence too.

### Slash Opening

The advantage of the slash opening is that the hand-sewn ladder stitch will be hidden on the inner side of the limbs. This method works best when the limb pattern is one piece with a fold in the back and a seam in the front. Select hardware that can be tightened from only one side.

1. With the wrong sides together, sew the inner and outer arms together without leaving an opening for stuffing. Repeat for the legs, inserting the foot pads.

2. To mark and cut the slash openings, first lay the legs in front of you, with inner side up and the toes pointing toward each other. Do both legs at once to be sure you create a left and right. Repeat for the arms (see fig. 54).

3. Beginning at the joint dot, draw a line straight down that is as long as the joint disk is wide.

4. Following the straight of grain, cut along the line. Be careful to cut through only one layer of fabric.

5. Turn the legs to the right side through the cut made in step 4. Repeat for the arms.

6. Stuff the limbs up to the bottom of the slash line.

7. At this point, assemble the joint hardware required for your project. See "Jointing" starting on page 44. Place the first half of the assembled joint through the slash, sliding the disk to the top of the slash. The disk will fill out the top of the limb. Keeping one side of the disk against the inner side of the leg or arm, stuff between the other side of the disk and the outer side of the limb.

8. When fully stuffed, sew the slash line closed with the ladder stitch (page 51) and bonded nylon thread. Tie off and bury the knot. Attach the limb to the bear body following the method required for your choice of hardware.

### Opening at Top of Limb

When the opening is at the top of the limb, the fabric on the outer portion of the limb is usually higher and wider than the fabric on the inner portion. The resulting seam is almost hidden because it is pulled slightly toward the inner portion of the limb and lies along the edge of the joint disk. Select hardware that can be tightened from only one side.

1.  Use an awl or the end of a sharp pair of scissors to make a hole at the joint mark. Turn the limb right side out, and stuff it three-quarters full.

2.  At this point, assemble the joint hardware required for your project. Place the hardware from the first half of the assembled joint through the joint hole. Keep the disk tight against the fabric and only place the stuffing toward the outer portion of the limb.

3.  When the limb is almost full, start sewing the top of the limb closed with a ladder stitch and bonded nylon thread. Ease the outer limb fabric to fit the inner edge. Add stuffing to fill the top of the limb as you sew.

4.  Tie off and bury the knot so that it does not show on the surface. Attach the limbs to the body following the method required for your choice of hardware.

### Opening Along the Seam on Limb

There are two differences between this opening and the opening at the top of the limb; otherwise, the procedure is the same. The first difference is the placement of the opening, which is generally on the side and close to the top of the limb. The second difference is that the pieces are the same size, so the seam will not be pulled one way or the other. You may use any jointing hardware with this opening.

### Ladder Stitch

Use a ladder stitch to sew the openings closed. Always work from the right side. With bonded nylon thread and a long needle, take a stitch through one layer of the fabric, the width of the seam allowance away from the cut edge. Cross over the opening to the other edge and take another stitch. Pull the thread tight and watch as the cut edges roll to the inside and disappear. Continue taking a stitch on alternate sides and pulling the thread tight after each stitch. As you sew the openings closed, you may need to add more stuffing.

To end the stitching, tie a knot on the surface and run the needle back into the same hole as the thread is in now. Bring the needle out at least 2" away from that hole. Pull the thread tight to bring the knot back through the hole to the inside. Keep pulling the thread tight, and cut it close to the fabric. The cut end of the thread will disappear under the fabric.

### Closing the Neck Opening

Follow the directions for the bear you are making to attach the head to the body. In most of the patterns in this book, you will leave the neck edge on the head open so that you can place the assembled joint hardware inside the head through the opening. To do this, stuff the head, leaving a little room to place the head joint

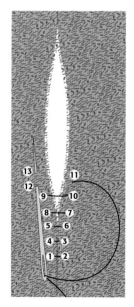

Ladder stitch

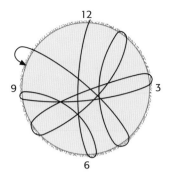

Fig. 55. Spider Web Stitch.
Pull thread tight after each stitch.

disk. Place the first half of the assembled joint into the head, with the cotter pin sticking out. Close the neck edge on the head with a "spider web" of stitches. To do this stitching technique, imagine the neck area as the face of a clock. Begin a stitch at 12, go down to 6, up to 9, and over to 3. Pull each stitch tight. Continue around the numbers until all the fabric lies flat. Tie off and bury the ends (see fig. 55).

## THREAD JOINTING

**Supplies:**
Long doll needle
Waxed thread

Thread jointing is the simplest of all the jointing systems and is used frequently on miniature and small bears. Buttons are sometimes sewn to the outside of the bear limbs, but this is optional. Stuff all the pieces and close the openings with a ladder stitch before jointing.

Fig.56

1.  Pin the head on top of the body. Thread a long needle with 2 strands of waxed thread that are five times longer than the height of the bear. Insert the needle at the top of the head and go through the head and body, leaving long tails of thread. Come out at one of the leg positions.

2.  Remove the needle from the thread. Thread the needle with the thread tails sticking out at the top of the head. Insert the threaded needle into the same hole at the top of the head. Go through the head and body again, making sure your needle goes down a different path once the needle is inside the stuffing. Be sure to insert the needle in the same exit hole each time so the thread does not show on the outside of the fabric. To do this, spread the 2 strands of thread far enough apart so that you can see the hole, and place the needle between the 2 strands. Exit the body at the opposite leg position. Pull the threads on each side of the body to make sure the head is attached straight on the body (see fig. 56).

3.  Pin the legs in position. Check their position by rotating them to stand and sit. Insert the threaded needle into the inside of the leg and come out on the outside of the leg. Go back into the same hole on the outside of the leg. If desired, add a button before you go back into the hole. Go back into the same hole through the body, exiting on the opposite side of the body and through the leg. Go back into the leg from the outside. Add a button to the outside of the limb if desired (see fig. 57).

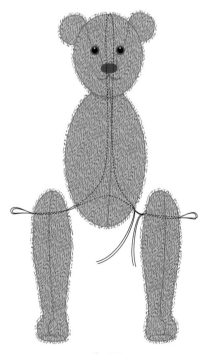

Fig. 57

4.  Pull the thread tight and make sure that the legs are in the right position. Then pull the thread tight again and tie it under one leg. Finally, pull the thread tail through the body to the opposite side before cutting the ends.

5. Pin the arms in position. Thread a needle with two 24"-long strands of thread. Insert the threaded needle into the arm joint mark on one side of the body and come out on the opposite side. Go through the inside of the arm and come out on the opposite side. Go back into the same hole on the outside of the arm, adding a button if desired. Go back into the body through the same hole, exiting on the opposite side of the body and into the inside of the other arm. Come out on the outside of the arm; then go back into the same hole, adding a button if desired. Pull the thread tight and make sure that the arms are in the right position. Then pull the thread tight again and tie it under one arm. Finally, pull the thread tail through the body to the opposite side before cutting the ends (see fig. 58).

## PLASTIC JOINTS

Plastic doll joints are available at most craft stores. They are a good choice for bears made for children because they are durable and washable. However, they come in a limited range of sizes, and they can be difficult to tighten because the bulk of the fur fabrics takes up too much space for the lock washer to fit onto the post correctly. However, by doubling the fabric between the washer and the post disk, it fills the loose space.

When installing plastic joints in synthetic knit-back fur, use the slash method for the opening.

1. Centering the slash on the limb where the disk will be, make a cut into the fur long enough to accommodate the disk.

2. Cut a small hole on each side of the opening.

3. Stuff the limb. Slip the disk into the slit. Insert the post into one of the holes.

4. Insert the post into the other hole (see fig. 59). No need to sew the opening closed. The slit will be secure and hidden between the joint disks. The added bulk also makes for a tighter joint.

## FLEXLIMBS

A Flexlimb is a foam-covered wire with a wire eyelet at one end. It is placed inside a bear limb and connected to the joint, making the limb flexible for posing. The pattern for the bear Billi on pages 68–73 is designed so that the foot and leg are all one piece. This type of leg allows you to bend the Flexlimb to form any size foot or point the toe. You may also use Flexlimbs in a leg with a foot pad. End the Flexlimb at the ankle or extend it into the toes. Note that if you straighten the Flexlimb in an arm that is too curved, the range of motion will be limited and it will place stress on the fabric.

Make an opening for stuffing at the top of the limb for easy access and assembly of the Flexlimb and joint. You can use other opening positions, but I find it is much easier to insert the Flexlimb when the opening is at the top of the limb. Flexlimbs need to be installed before stuffing.

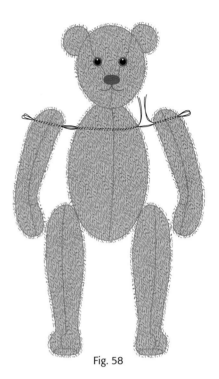

**Fig. 58**

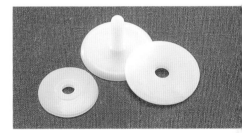

Plastic joints

Fig 59. Insert the post into both holes.

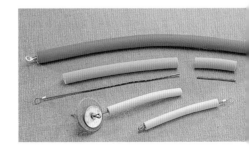

Flexlimbs are available in several sizes.

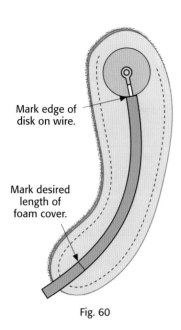

Mark edge of disk on wire.

Mark desired length of foam cover.

Fig. 60

## Adjusting Length

1. With limb wrong side out and inner limb facing up, position the wire eyelet and the disk hole over the joint mark. Move the foam cover down, just below the edge of the disk. Mark the position of the edge of the disk on the wire. With the foam cover still below the edge of the disk, mark the total desired length on the foam cover (see fig. 60). Remove the foam cover from the wire. Cut the foam at length mark. The length of the Flexlimb should fit as far into the arm as possible without stressing the fabric.

2. Put the foam cover back on the wire and mark the total desired length on the wire. Add ½"–1" and make another mark. Cut the wire at this mark (see fig. 61).

3. Move the foam cover up as far as possible. Bend the wire at the desired length mark, forming a loop (see fig. 62). Slide the foam cover down to cover the loop end. Flatten the loop if necessary, but not too much since the width of the loop will prevent the foam from sliding beyond the wire end.

4. Turn the limb right side out. Place a small amount of stuffing in the paw and foot to cushion the wire end.

## Assembly

1. Cut a tiny hole at the limb joint mark. Place the Flexlimb inside the limb through the top opening and assemble the joint as follows: On the cotter pin, place a small washer, a fender washer, wire eyelet (flat side against the disk) hardboard disk, and wrong side of limb fabric.

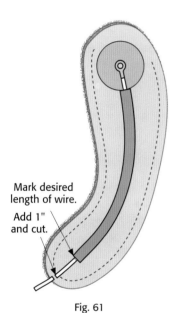

Mark desired length of wire.

Add 1" and cut.

Fig. 61

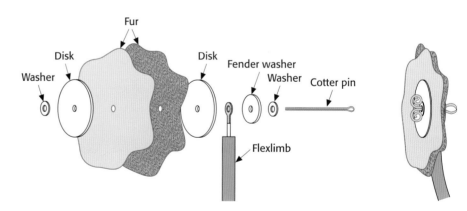

Washer · Disk · Fur · Disk · Fender washer · Washer · Cotter pin · Flexlimb

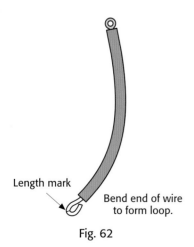

Length mark

Bend end of wire to form loop.

Fig. 62

2. Lightly stuff limbs with plastic or glass pellets or high-loft polyester. Do not overstuff. Test to be sure that the stuffing does not restrict the bendability of the Flexlimb. Stuff the top of the limb. Close the opening with a ladder stitch, pulling the stitches tight and easing in the fullness. Tie off and bury knots.

3. Place the cotter pin legs through the hole in the body. From inside the body, place the other disk and washer onto the cotter pin. Use a cotter key or needle-nose pliers to curl the ends of the cotter pin and tighten the joint.

# Music Box and Waggie Shaft

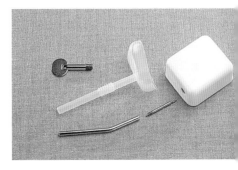

Waggie Shaft and music box parts

THE WAGGIE SHAFT is a post that extends from a music box into the head of a bear. When the music box is playing, the Waggie Shaft turns, causing the head to move in time with the music. It works best in bears from 10" to 16" tall. The turn key to the music box will stick out of the back seam. To play the music box, wind the key clockwise. Do not over wind, and do not try to remove the child-safe key or it may damage the music box.

To assemble the Waggie Shaft and music box:

1. Screw the threaded end of the small adapter shaft counterclockwise into the bent-metal Waggie Shaft. Then push the other end into the adapter hole on top of the music box.

2. Slip the plastic cover over the Waggie Shaft and the top of the music box.

Assembled music box and Waggie Shaft

Installing the unit in jointed bears:

1. Stuff the muzzle firmly. Leave a hole in the back of the head for stuffing. Attach arms and legs. Make the joint holes in the body neck and head large enough for the Waggie Shaft. If the neck edges are not sewn closed, use "spider web" stitches (see page 52) to gather the edges to fit the Waggie Shaft.

2. Place the assembled Waggie Shaft and music box in the body and head so that the music box fills the shoulders and the bend in the shaft clears the neck (see fig. 63).

3. Sew the head onto the shoulders with a running stitch. The head will move better if the stitches form a smaller circle than the disk size normally used in your bear pattern.

4. Finish stuffing. Do not overstuff the head and neck. Overstuffing will prevent the Waggie Shaft from moving. And do not stuff between the back of the music box (sound board) and fabric or the music will be hard to hear.

5. Insert the turn key into the music box. Sew the openings closed with a ladder stitch.

Fig. 63

# Tilt Growler

A TILT GROWLER will give your bear a voice. It is a device that makes a noise when you shake or move the bear. Choose one that will fit inside the tummy of the bear and still allow room for ample stuffing. If the growler does not have a protective covering over the sound holes, make a small cloth bag large enough to hold the growler. Sew the ends of the bag closed. If the sound holes are not protected, the stuffing may migrate into the growler and damage it.

Place the growler inside the body with the sound holes against the tummy fabric. Place stuffing around the growler to hold it in place. Do not put any stuffing between the growler and the tummy fabric or the sound will be muffled.

Example of tilt growlers with protective covers

# CLAWS

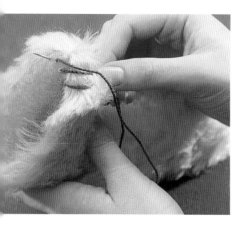

Stitching claws

YOU CAN STITCH claws on both the paw pads and foot pads.

1.  Thread an 18" length of perle cotton on a long needle and knot one end.

2.  Insert the needle into the back seam line on the leg. Place the needle between the stitches instead of through the fabric. If it won't go, the needle is probably caught on the fabric. Remove the perle cotton and start again.

3.  Exit the needle through the foot pad, about ¼" below the seam between the fur and foot pad. Pull the perle cotton until the knot pulls through the seam. Insert the needle into the top of the foot, about 1" from the seam. This is the first claw.

4.  Exit through the foot pad, again about ¼" below the seam and about ¼" away from the previous claw. Insert the needle into the top of the foot, about 1" from the seam, or the length suited to your bear, and about ¼" away from the previous stitch. This is the second claw.

5.  Repeat to make 3 more claws, spacing them evenly around the front of the foot pad.

6.  To finish, exit through the back leg seam and then insert the needle in the same exact spot. This tangles the perle cotton in the stuffing enough to hold it in place. Exit through the fabric at least 2" away, pull the thread tight, and cut.

# BEAR ACCESSORIES

EACH BEAR YOU make will have its own personality. And while you may have some control over this personality by how you place the ears, eyes, nose, and mouth, you'll soon discover that most bears have subtle ways of letting you know exactly who they want to be—shy or bold, casual or distinguished.

Once you finish making the bear, you can leave the bear as it is or you can enhance its personality by dressing the bear in clothes or adding simple accessories. Six of the bears in this book have directions and patterns for simple outfits. Clothing can be as simple as an elegant bow tied around the neck or as elaborate as a dress trimmed in lace with shoes to match. If you're a knitter, try knitting a small sweater.

If you don't want to clothe your bear, you can add a pair of glasses made from thin wire for a scholarly look, or a fishing pole made from a twig for a fisherman bear. You can also use accessories to capture a favorite pastime or celebrate a special occasion. Look for items in toy stores, antique shops, or doll shops. Once you start looking for ways to accessorize you bear, you'll be surprised at all the things you can make or buy.

# BEAR PROJECTS

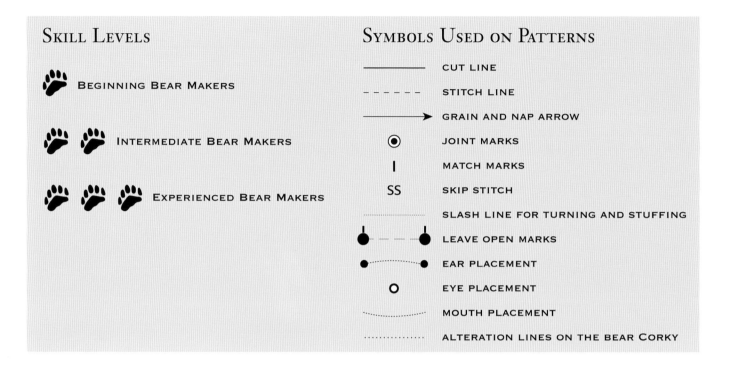

**SKILL LEVELS**

BEGINNING BEAR MAKERS

INTERMEDIATE BEAR MAKERS

EXPERIENCED BEAR MAKERS

**SYMBOLS USED ON PATTERNS**

| | |
|---|---|
| ——————— | CUT LINE |
| - - - - - - | STITCH LINE |
| ———————▶ | GRAIN AND NAP ARROW |
| ⊙ | JOINT MARKS |
| I | MATCH MARKS |
| SS | SKIP STITCH |
| ·············· | SLASH LINE FOR TURNING AND STUFFING |
| ●- - -● | LEAVE OPEN MARKS |
| ●·········● | EAR PLACEMENT |
| O | EYE PLACEMENT |
| ‿ | MOUTH PLACEMENT |
| ················ | ALTERATION LINES ON THE BEAR CORKY |

*R*EAD THROUGH ALL the directions before starting your bear. Keep the following pointers in mind as you construct your bear.

* Make a copy of the pattern pieces and transfer all markings to the pattern pieces.
* Lay the pattern pieces on the wrong side of the fur fabric, following the nap and grain line arrows.
* Pin the pattern pieces to the fabric, or trace around the pattern pieces.
* Use small, sharp scissors to cut through the backing fabric only.
* Follow the recommended seam allowance. Most bears are sewn with ¼"-wide seam allowances. However, a few are sewn with ⅛" seam allowances.
* With right sides together, align match marks, pin pieces together, tucking fur inside before sewing. Sew from cut edge to cut edge, unless otherwise instructed.
* Use all-purpose sewing thread for machine sewing all bears.
* Use all-purpose sewing thread for hand sewing small bears. Coat thread with beeswax to prevent wear on thread.
* Use bonded nylon thread for hand sewing medium to large bears, and for gathering neck edges.
* Groom seams before turning to right side.
* Hard stuff the muzzle for the best embroidered nose.
* Use waxed thread for installing eyes.
* Close all openings with bonded nylon thread and a ladder stitch, unless otherwise instructed.

# CHIP  *This is an easy bear for a beginner, with an easy-to-hide stuffing hole.*

BEAR FACTS: THE FIRST TEDDY BEAR MADE AND SOLD IN THE U.S. WAS MADE BY MORRIS AND ROSE MICHTOM, A RUSSIAN IMMIGRANT COUPLE LIVING IN BROOKLYN, NEW YORK. THEY OWNED A CANDY AND TOY SHOP AND FOUNDED THE IDEAL NOVELTY AND TOY COMPANY.

*8½" Jointed Bear by Linda Mead, 1999, Spare Bear Parts, Interlochen, Michigan*

# MATERIALS

* 9" x 12" square of ⅛"-pile mohair fur fabric
* 1½" x 2½" piece of velvet for paw pads
* 1 pair of 4 mm onyx beads for eyes
* Size 5 perle cotton for nose and mouth
* Firm-pack polyester stuffing
* Cotter-pin joints
  * Five ¾" disks for head and legs
  * Five ½" disks for neck and arms
  * 10 cotter-pin washers
  * Five 1¼" cotter pins

# DIRECTIONS

*All seam allowances are ⅛".*

Refer to "Getting Started" on pages 21–24 for making the patterns, cutting fabric, and transferring markings. To machine sew the narrow seams on small bear pattern pieces that are mirror images and do not have darts (arms, legs, and ears), see "Sewing Small Bears" on page 26.

**ARMS:** Pin and sew paw pad to inner arm at wrist edge, matching A marks. Fold arm right sides together, match all marks, and pin. Sew around arm without leaving an opening. Repeat for other arm.

**LEGS:** Fold leg right sides together, match all marks, and pin. Starting at heel, sew around leg without leaving an opening. Repeat for other leg.

**BODY:** Sew darts at top and bottom of body pieces. Pin body halves together, matching all marks. Starting at front neck edge, sew down front and around bottom to "Leave open" mark on lower back. Sew from back neck edge down to upper to "Leave open" mark.

**HEAD WITH TRIANGLE MUZZLE** (page 29): Pin head gusset to a side head piece, matching all marks. With head gusset on top, sew from B to end of gusset, leaving one side open as marked. Repeat with other side head piece. Pin side heads together along neck, and sew from back of neck, across neck, and up to nose (B). Use contrasting thread for tailor tacks to mark ear and eye placements on outside of head.

Insert a ¾" disk and cotter pin inside head. Stuff head, packing the muzzle area firmly. As you stuff, mold the face with your hands. Close opening with a ladder stitch.

**EARS:** Pin and sew 2 ear pieces together along curved edges, leaving straight edges open. Repeat for other ear.

## ARTIST TIP

If the fabric becomes tangled and won't move easily when turning small limbs to the right side, place closed forceps into the tangled folds of the fabric and spread the forceps open to straighten the fabric. Repeat several times until the fabric slides freely again.

## ABOUT THE PATTERN

The leg and arm pattern pieces are marked with a slash line that extends below the joint mark. Making the opening for turning, stuffing, and jointing on the inner side of the limbs allows you to hide the hand sewing used to close the limb.

**LIMB JOINTS:** Referring to "Slash Opening" on page 50, cut along slash line on arms and legs. Use forceps to turn pieces right side out (see page 31). Referring to "Cotter-Pin Joints" on pages 46–47, attach limbs to body. Stuff arms and legs and close openings.

**NECK JOINT:** Gather neck edge on body and insert the legs of the cotter pin from head into the center of the gathered neck. Place a ½" disk on a cotter pin inside body and curl cotter pin as instructed for limbs above. Stuff body and close opening.

**FACE:** Referring to pages 35–44, install eyes, trim muzzle, embroider nose and mouth, and attach ears.

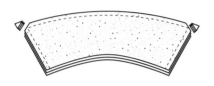

Topstitch ⅛" from edge.

Zigzag raw edges.

Fig. 64

Fold line

Fig. 65

Fig. 66

Fold collar with stitching inside.

Hand stitch ends together.

Fig. 67

# COLLAR AND TIE

## MATERIALS

* 6" square of white fabric for collar
* 3" x 6" piece of medium-weight interfacing for collar
* 8" square of plaid fabric for tie
* 3" x 7" piece of lightweight interfacing for tie

1. With right sides of fabric together and interfacing on top, stitch around three sides of collar with a ⅛" seam allowance. Trim corners, turn collar to right side, and press. Topstitch ⅛" around edge of collar. Zigzag raw edges together (see fig. 64).

2. For tie, cut a 1¼" x 6" strip of fabric for neck strap. With wrong sides together, fold fabric in half lengthwise and press. Fold cut edges to meet first fold and press (see fig. 65). Neck strap should be ⅜" x 6". Set aside.

3. With right sides of fabric together and lightweight interfacing on top, stitch all around tie edges. Cut slash line on interfacing and one layer of fabric. Trim corners, turn to right side, and press. Attach tie to center of neck strap with a half-hitch knot. Keep narrow end of tie shorter and behind the wide end (see fig. 66).

4. Fold collar in half lengthwise. Place around neck of bear so that top half of collar covers raw edges and front edges meet in the middle; hand stitch in place (see fig. 67).

5. Position tie in front, placing neck strap under fold of collar. Hand stitch ends of neck strap in place at back of bear, under the fold of the collar.

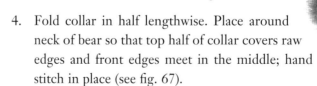

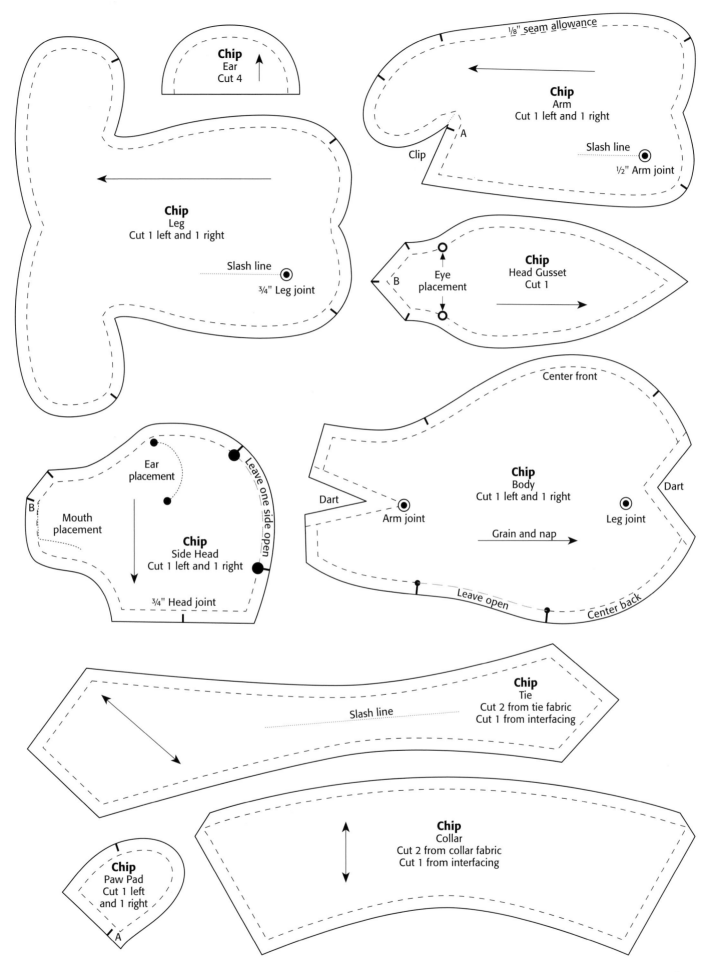

**Chip**
Ear
Cut 4

¹⁄₈" seam allowance

**Chip**
Arm
Cut 1 left and 1 right

Clip

A

Slash line

¹⁄₂" Arm joint

**Chip**
Leg
Cut 1 left and 1 right

Slash line

³⁄₄" Leg joint

B

Eye placement

**Chip**
Head Gusset
Cut 1

Center front

Ear placement

Mouth placement

B

**Chip**
Side Head
Cut 1 left and 1 right

Leave one side open

³⁄₄" Head joint

Dart

Arm joint

**Chip**
Body
Cut 1 left and 1 right

Leg joint

Dart

Grain and nap

Leave open

Center back

Slash line

**Chip**
Tie
Cut 2 from tie fabric
Cut 1 from interfacing

**Chip**
Collar
Cut 2 from collar fabric
Cut 1 from interfacing

**Chip**
Paw Pad
Cut 1 left
and 1 right

A

# OLD WORLD BEAR

 *Learn the techniques of old-world teddy bear companies.*

BEAR FACTS: AFTER THEIR FIRST INTRODUCTION, TEDDY BEARS QUICKLY BECAME FAVORITE TOYS IN THE U.S. AT THE END OF 1903, STEIFF, THE FAMOUS GERMAN BEAR MANUFACTURER, HAD SOLD 12,000 TEDDIES. BY THE END OF 1907, THEY HAD SOLD 974,000!

*15½" Center Seam, Jointed Bear by Linda Mead, 1999, Spare Bear Parts, Interlochen, Michigan*

# MATERIALS

* ★ Fat quarter (18" x 26") of ¾"-pile mohair fur fabric
* ★ 5" x 8" piece of felt for paw pads and foot pads
* ★ Size 3 perle cotton for nose and mouth
* ★ Beeswax for nose
* ★ 1 pair of 14 mm black glass eyes
* ★ Excelsior stuffing
* ★ Firm-pack polyester stuffing (optional)
* ★ Cotter-pin joints
  * Two 2¼" joint disks for head and neck
  * Four 1¾" disks for legs
  * Four 1½" disks for arms
  * 10 cotter-pin washers
  * Five 2" cotter pins

# DIRECTIONS

*All seam allowances are ¼".*

Refer to "Getting Started" on pages 21–24 for making patterns, cutting fabric, and transferring markings. Refer to the pattern layout on page 64 before cutting pieces. To make a full leg pattern, place the pattern piece on the fold of a piece of paper, trace, and cut out.

**GROOMING SEAMS:** If you prefer an old-looking bear, do not pull the fur out of the seams after sewing.

**ARMS:** Pin and sew paw pad to inner arm at wrist edge, matching A marks. Fold arm right sides together, match all marks, and pin. Sew around arm, leaving an opening as marked. Repeat for other arm.

**LEGS:** Fold leg right sides together, match all marks, and pin. Starting at toe, sew around leg to top, leaving an opening as marked. Match and pin toe mark on foot pad to toe seam of leg. Match and pin heel mark on foot pad to heel mark on leg. Pin foot pad to each side of leg. Place additional pins between these 4 pins as needed to keep raw edges of foot pad and leg even and the fullness equally distributed. With the foot pad on top, sew around foot. Refer to "Foot Pads" on page 28 for additional guidance. Repeat for other leg.

**BODY:** Pin 1 front and 1 back piece together at side seam, matching all marks. Sew from neck edge to bottom corner. Repeat for the other side with remaining front and back pieces. Pin the 2 body halves together, matching all marks. Starting at "Leave open" mark on upper back, sew around hump, down front, and around bottom to "Leave open" mark on lower back.

## ABOUT THE PATTERN

This bear pattern is designed in the tradition of the early teddy bear manufacturing companies—Steiff, Bing, and Farnell. In addition to the pattern design, the assembly techniques and materials used also follow these vintage styles and methods, which I have learned while repairing vintage bears.

One of these methods, the pieced head gusset, resulted from early bear manufacturers not wanting to waste expensive mohair. The Steiff company used leftover fabric next to the selvage by piecing the head gusset, cutting the pattern lengthwise from the nose to the back of the head. This created today's collectible bear, often referred to as the "center seam Steiff." The seam runs the length of the head gusset along the grain line, making the head center more stable and less stretchable when the bear's head is packed hard with stuffing.

In addition to a distinct head gusset, vintage bears often lack seams that are groomed from the wrong side. The old bears were made for use as toys and time was not spent on such details. To imitate this characteristic, I left just enough seam fur poking up through the muzzle center stitch line of Old World Bear to attract attention to the center seam feature.

**HEAD WITH ROUNDED MUZZLE** (page 30): Pin and sew head gusset pieces together along straight edge. Pin side-head pieces together, matching all marks. Sew from nose (B), down chin to front neck. Pin head gusset to a side head piece, matching all marks. With gusset on top, sew from nose (B) to end of gusset (C). Repeat with other side head piece. Leave neck edge open. Use contrasting thread for tailor tacks to mark ear and eye placements on outside of head.

**EARS:** Pin and sew 2 ear pieces together along curved edges, leaving straight edges open. Repeat for other ear.

**STUFFING AND JOINTING:** Stuff head and limbs with excelsior to create a reproduction of a vintage bear. Attach head and limbs to body, referring to "Cotter-Pin Joints" on page 46, and "Closing the Neck Opening" on page 51. Stuff body and close openings.

**FACE:** Referring to pages 35–44, install eyes, trim muzzle, embroider nose and mouth, and attach ears.

**OPTIONAL:** Wax perle cotton before embroidering nose and mouth. Use a piece of sandpaper on the black glass eyes to dull the finish and to duplicate the look of old leather shoe buttons, which were used as eyes on vintage teddy bears.

**CLAWS:** Referring to "Claws" on page 56, embroider claws on paw pads and foot pads.

**FINISHING:** Tie a ribbon around the neck, if desired. Give your new bear a big hug!

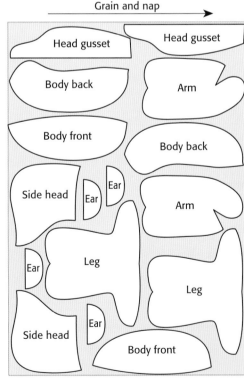

Grain and nap

Head gusset · Head gusset · Body back · Arm · Body front · Body back · Side head · Ear · Ear · Arm · Ear · Leg · Leg · Side head · Ear · Body front

**Pattern layout**

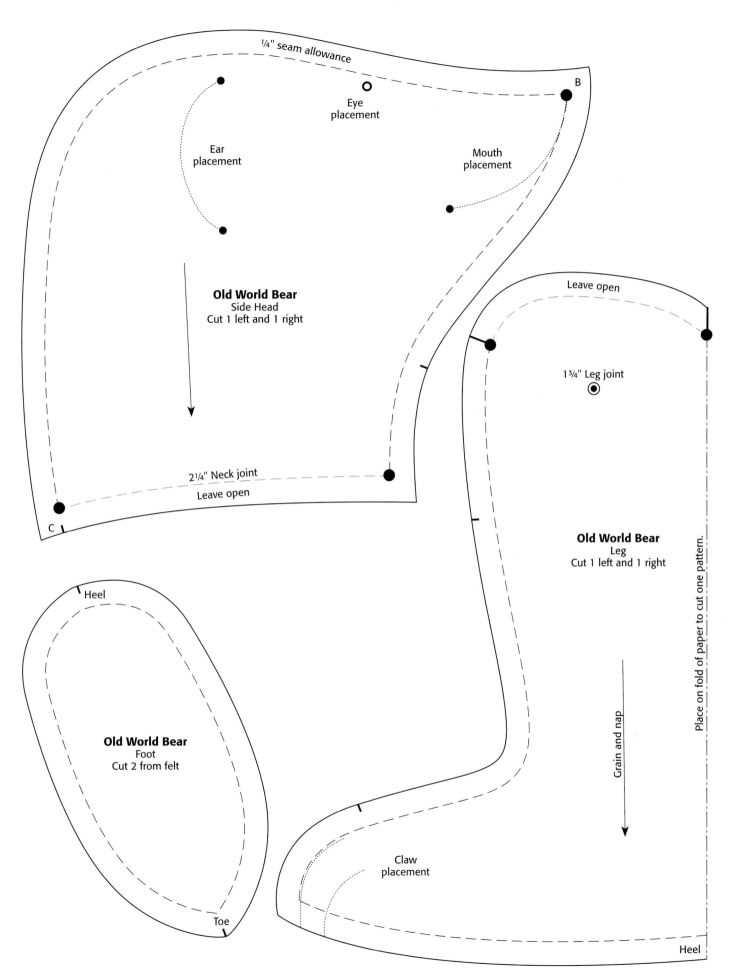

¼" seam allowance

Eye
placement

B

Ear
placement

Mouth
placement

**Old World Bear**
Side Head
Cut 1 left and 1 right

Leave open

1¾" Leg joint

2¼" Neck joint

Leave open

C

**Old World Bear**
Leg
Cut 1 left and 1 right

Heel

Place on fold of paper to cut one pattern.

**Old World Bear**
Foot
Cut 2 from felt

Grain and nap

Claw
placement

Toe

Heel

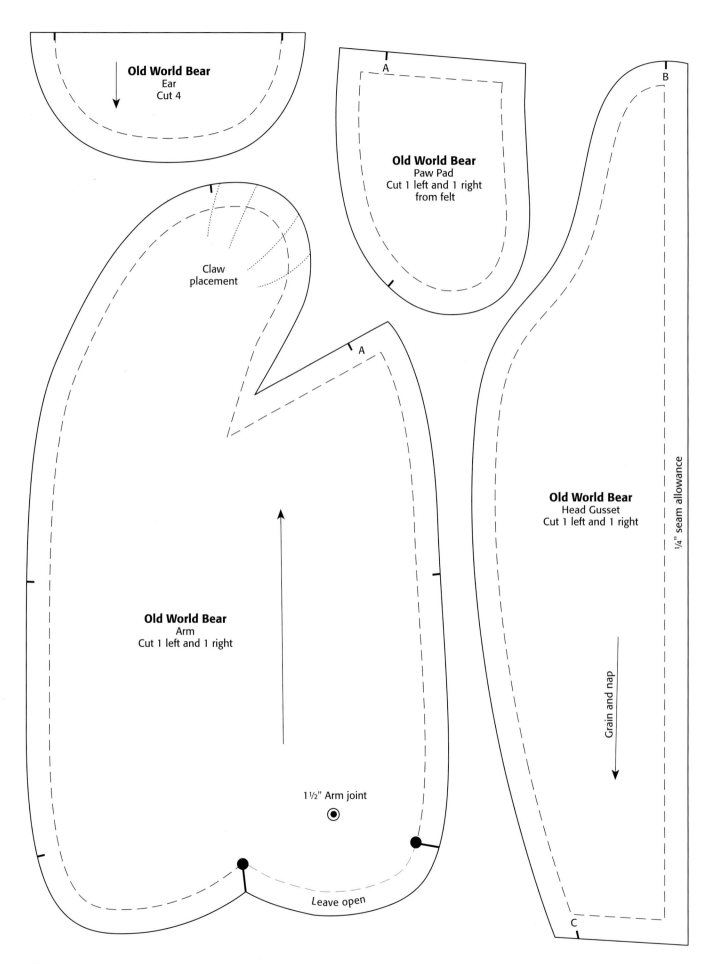

**Old World Bear**
Ear
Cut 4

A

**Old World Bear**
Paw Pad
Cut 1 left and 1 right
from felt

B

Claw
placement

A

**Old World Bear**
Head Gusset
Cut 1 left and 1 right

¼" seam allowance

**Old World Bear**
Arm
Cut 1 left and 1 right

Grain and nap

1½" Arm joint

Leave open

C

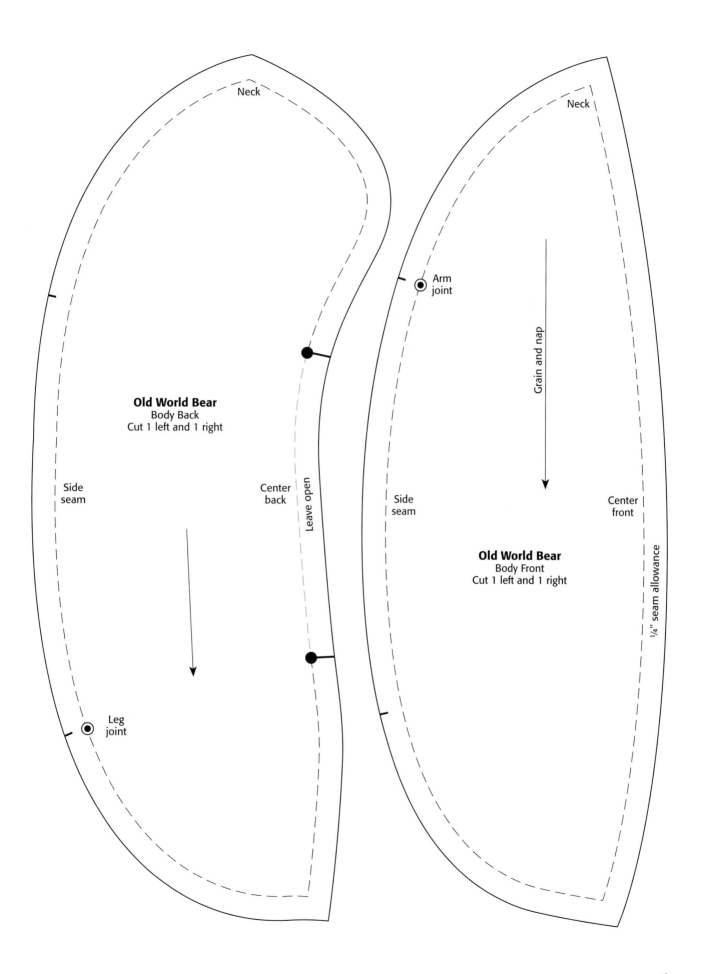

Neck

**Old World Bear**
Body Back
Cut 1 left and 1 right

Side
seam

Center
back

Leave open

Leg
joint

Neck

Arm
joint

Grain and nap

Side
seam

Center
front

**Old World Bear**
Body Front
Cut 1 left and 1 right

¼" seam allowance

# BILLI

 *Make this bear without Flexlimbs.*

 *Make this bear with Flexlimbs.*

BEAR FACTS: SMOKEY THE BEAR WAS CREATED FOR THE U.S. FORESTRY DEPARTMENT IN 1944 FOR A POSTER ENCOURAGING FIRE SAFETY. THE IDEAL TOY COMPANY WAS THE FIRST TO MANUFACTURE SMOKEY AS A STUFFED TOY.

*15" Jointed Bear by Sandy Sabo, 1998, VitoBear Company, Crystal Lake, Illinois*

# MATERIALS

* ⅓ yd. of ¾"-pile mohair
* 1 pair of 12 mm black glass eyes
* Size 5 perle cotton for nose and mouth
* Firm-pack polyester stuffing
* Plastic pellets (optional)
* 1½" plastic safety joints for beginner bear maker

* Optional Flexlimb and cotter-pin joints for intermediate bear maker
    * Ten 1½" disks
    * 5 cotter-pin washers
    * Five 1½" cotter pins
    * 4 standard-weight Flexlimbs, each 8" x ⅝"
    * 4 fender washers for Flexlimbs

# DIRECTIONS

*All seam allowances are ¼".*

Refer to "Getting Started" on pages 21–24 for making patterns, cutting fabric, and transferring markings.

**GROOMING SEAMS:** After sewing each seam, pull fur out of seams on both wrong and right sides.

**ARMS:** Pin 2 arm pieces together, matching all marks. Sew around arm, leaving an opening as marked. Repeat for other arm.

**LEGS:** Pin 2 leg pieces together, matching all marks. Sew around leg, leaving an opening as marked. Repeat for other leg.

**BODY:** Pin and sew 2 body pieces together, leaving an opening as marked.

## ARTIST TIP

Trimming the fur high above the eyes will give the bear a sweet, innocent look.

## ABOUT THE PATTERN

Billi was designed by Sandy Sabo, a Spare Bear Parts Certified Instructor, as an easy project for a beginning bear maker. Use plastic joints if Billi will be your first bear project or if you are teaching a child how to make this bear. Plastic joints are easy to install and safe for your child.

For intermediate bear makers, Billi is a good pattern to learn how to install Flexlimbs. Flexlimbs are foam covered wires that are attached to the joints, making it possible to bend your bear's limbs and hold them in any position. Flexlimbs work well with a no-foot pad design like Billi, because designs with a formed foot and angled ankle restrict the range of motion of the limb.

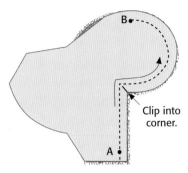

Fig. 68. Sew back side head and front side head together.

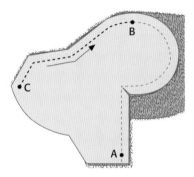

Fig. 69. Sew gusset to side head from nose to ear.

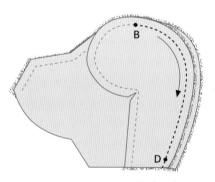

Fig. 70. Sew gusset to side head from ear to back of head.

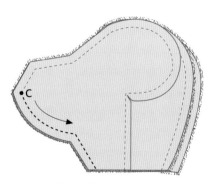

Fig. 71. Sew chin seam.

HEAD: The head consists of 2 front and 2 back side-head pieces and 1 head gusset. The ear is part of the side-head pieces. Pin front side head to back side head, matching A and B marks. Sew from A to B around the ear to make one complete side head. Repeat to make another complete side head. Clip into the corner (see fig. 68).

Pin head gusset to a side piece, matching B and C marks and easing to fit as needed. With the side head piece on top and the ear folded toward back of head, sew from C to beginning of stitching at B for ear; stop and backstitch (see fig. 69).

Remove the pieces from the machine. Fold the ear toward the nose, and resume sewing at B, backstitch, and continue to the end of the gusset at D. Repeat for second side, also with side head piece on top. Careful pinning and fitting is essential for a good head shape (see fig. 70).

Pin and sew the chin seam from C to front neck. Leave neck edge open (see fig. 71).

STUFFING: Stuff the head firmly with firm-pack polyester stuffing, referring to pages 34–35. Do not stuff ears. Refer to "Closing the Neck Opening" on pages 51–52. Use plastic pellets or a mix of pellets and polyester stuffing for limbs with or without Flexlimbs.

JOINTING: For first-time bear makers or for children, install plastic joints, referring to page 53. Refer to "Cotter-Pin Joints" on pages 46–47 and "Flexlimbs" on pages 53–54 if you are installing them.

FACE: Referring to pages 35–44, install eyes, trim muzzle, and embroider triangle nose and mouth.

# HAT AND SCARF

PURCHASE A READY-MADE doll hat and scarf to dress your bear, or recycle a colorful child's sweater to make a hat and scarf. For a hat, cut a 5" x 13" strip from the ribbed edge of a sweater. Sew the short ends together. Sew a running stitch along the cut edge of the strip and gather the edges tightly. Tie off threads securely. Turn right side out (see fig. 72).

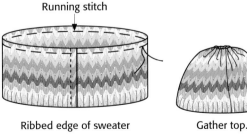

Running stitch

Ribbed edge of sweater                    Gather top.

Fig. 72

For scarf, cut sleeves off sweater body and cut sleeves open. Then cut straight up from cuff on both sides to square off the top of sleeves. Sew squared-off ends together; then sew along the length of sleeve. Turn right side out through cuff opening (see fig. 73). Presto—your bear is ready for a day in the snow!

Trim sleeves.

Join cut ends.

Sew long edges together.

Fig. 73

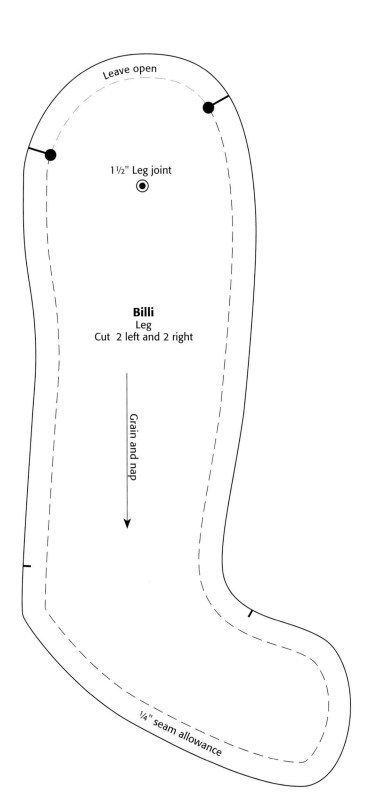

Leave open

1½" Leg joint

**Billi**
Leg
Cut  2 left and 2 right

Grain and nap

¼" seam allowance

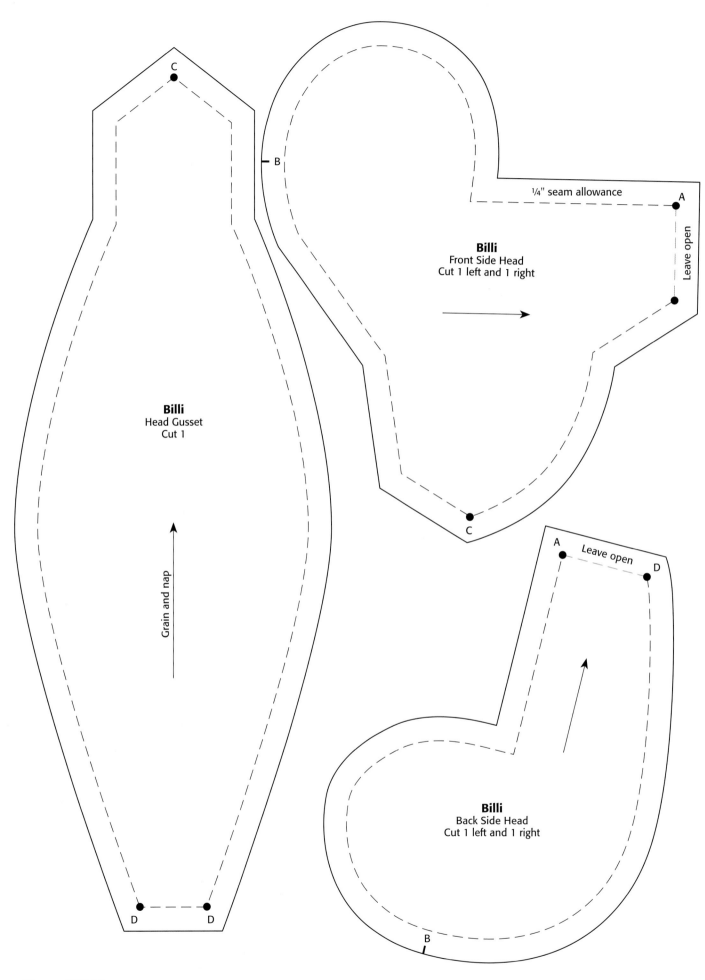

C

B —

¼" seam allowance    • A

**Billi**
Front Side Head
Cut 1 left and 1 right

→

Leave open

•

C

**Billi**
Head Gusset
Cut 1

Grain and nap

D    D

A    Leave open    D
•    •

**Billi**
Back Side Head
Cut 1 left and 1 right

B

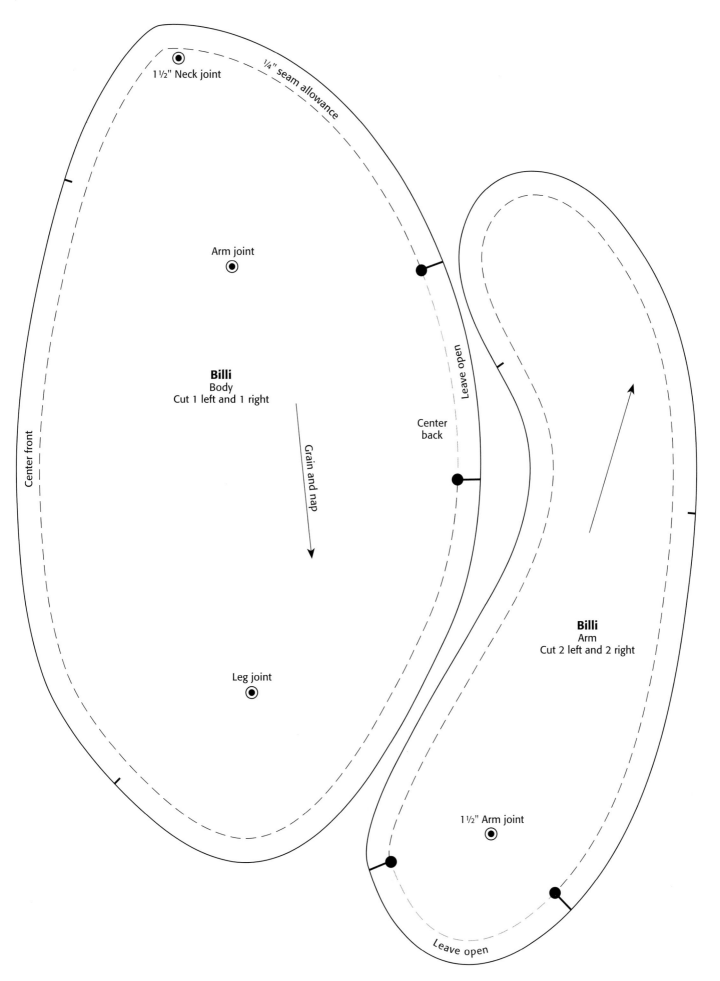

1½" Neck joint

¼" seam allowance

Arm joint

**Billi**
Body
Cut 1 left and 1 right

Grain and nap

Center front

Center back

Leave open

Leave open

**Billi**
Arm
Cut 2 left and 2 right

1½" Arm joint

Leg joint

Leave open

# SASHA  🐾 🐾  *Learn to install a music box and Waggie Shaft.*

**BEAR FACTS:**

• "TEDDY BEARS' PICNIC" MAY BE THOUGHT OF AS THE TEDDY BEAR THEME SONG, BUT THERE ARE MANY OTHER SONGS ABOUT THE TEDDY BEAR. "I WISH I HAD A TEDDY BEAR," "TEDDY'S COMING HOME," AND "THE TEDDY BEAR TWO-STEP" GO BACK TO THE EARLY 1900S. MORE RECENTLY, WE HAVE "LET ME BE YOUR TEDDY BEAR" BY ELVIS PRESLEY.

• IN 1928, THE U.S. TRADE MAGAZINE *TOY WORLD* STATED HELVETIC MANUFACTURED A SQUEEZE MUSIC BOX TEDDY BEAR.

*15" Jointed Bear by Linda Hartzig, 1999, What Else But Bears, Harrisburg, North Carolina*

# MATERIALS

* ¼ yd. of ¾"-pile mohair fur fabric
* 5" x 8" piece of wool felt for paw pads and foot pads
* 1 pair of 10 mm black glass eyes
* Size 5 pearl cotton for nose and mouth
* Excelsior to stuff muzzle
* Firm-pack polyester stuffing
* Nut and bolt joints
  * Four 2" joint disks for legs
  * Four 1¾" joint disks for arms
  * 4 bolts
  * 4 locknuts
* 1 Waggie Shaft
* 1 music box

If not installing a music box and Waggie Shaft you will also need:
  * Two 2" joint disks for head and neck
  * 1 bolt
  * 1 locknut

# DIRECTIONS

*All seam allowances are ¼".*

Refer to "Getting Started" on pages 21–24 for making patterns, cutting fabric, and transferring markings.

**GROOMING SEAMS:** After sewing each seam, pull fur out of seams on both wrong and right sides.

**EARS:** Linda Hartzig likes to start with the bear ears to get the feeling of sewing on the mohair, as each piece of mohair can be different. Pin and sew 2 ear pieces together along curved edges, leaving straight edges open. Repeat for other ear.

**ARMS:** Pin and sew paw pad to inner arm at wrist edge, matching mark. Pin inner arm to outer arm, matching all marks. Sew around arm, leaving an opening as marked. Repeat for other arm.

**LEGS:** Pin 2 legs together, matching all marks. Starting at toe, sew around leg to heel, leaving an opening as marked. Then match and pin toe mark on foot pad to toe seam of leg. Match and pin heel mark on foot pad to heel seam on leg. Pin foot pad to each side of leg. Place additional pins between these 4 pins as needed to keep the raw edges of foot pad and leg even and the fullness equally distributed. With the foot pad on top, sew around foot. Refer to "Foot Pads" on page 28. Repeat for other leg.

ARTIST TIP

To leave a pocket for the Waggie Shaft, place a pencil in the neck before you stuff the head; then pack stuffing around it.

ABOUT THE PATTERN

Sasha was designed by Linda Hartzig, Spare Bear Parts Certified Instructor, as an easy jointed bear for beginners. If you prefer, you can install a music box, use a Waggie Shaft for the neck joint, and watch Sasha move her head to the music.

**BODY:** Pin 2 body pieces together, matching all marks. Sew around body, leaving an opening at back and neck as marked.

**HEAD WITH ROUNDED MUZZLE** (page 30): Pin side head pieces together, matching A and B marks. Sew chin seam from A to B. Pin head gusset to a side head piece, matching all marks. With gusset on top, sew from nose (A) to back of gusset. Repeat with other side head piece, also with gusset on top. Finish seam from end of gusset to the neck edge, if necessary.

**STUFFING AND JOINTING:** Stuff muzzle with excelsior. Use firm-pack polyester for the rest of the head. Attach limbs and head (if not installing Waggie Shaft) to body, referring to "Locknut and Bolt (or Tap-Bolt) Joints" on pages 47–48. Stuff limbs and body and close openings.

To install music box and Waggie Shaft, refer to page 55. As you stuff head, place an unsharpened pencil into neck opening and firmly stuff around it. Close neck opening around pencil with a gather stitch. Leave pencil in head until you are ready to attach head to body.

**FACE:** Referring to "Creating the Face" on pages 35–44, install eyes, embroider nose and mouth, and attach ears.

# SKATING SKIRT

## MATERIALS

* 9" x 12" piece of upholstery velvet (non-ravel fabric)
* Velcro
* Optional laces, ribbons, fur, and buttons to decorate skirt
* Optional pair of doll ice skates; see "Resources" on pages 152–153

1. Refer to fig. 74. Cut 1 skirt on the fold of fabric as marked on pattern. Sew short ends of skirt together, stitching 1" from bottom of skirt as shown on pattern; backstitch at both ends of seam. If you choose a fabric that will ravel, add ¼" before cutting to the bottom of the skirt for a hem. Hand stitch a rolled hem.

2. Cut 1 strip, ⅝" x 12", for waistband. Topstitch waistband to skirt. Sew Velcro at waistband to close. Decorate skirt with lace, ribbon, fur, and buttons as desired.

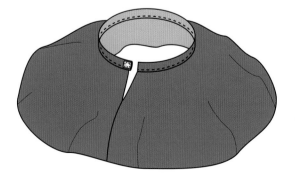

**Fig. 74**

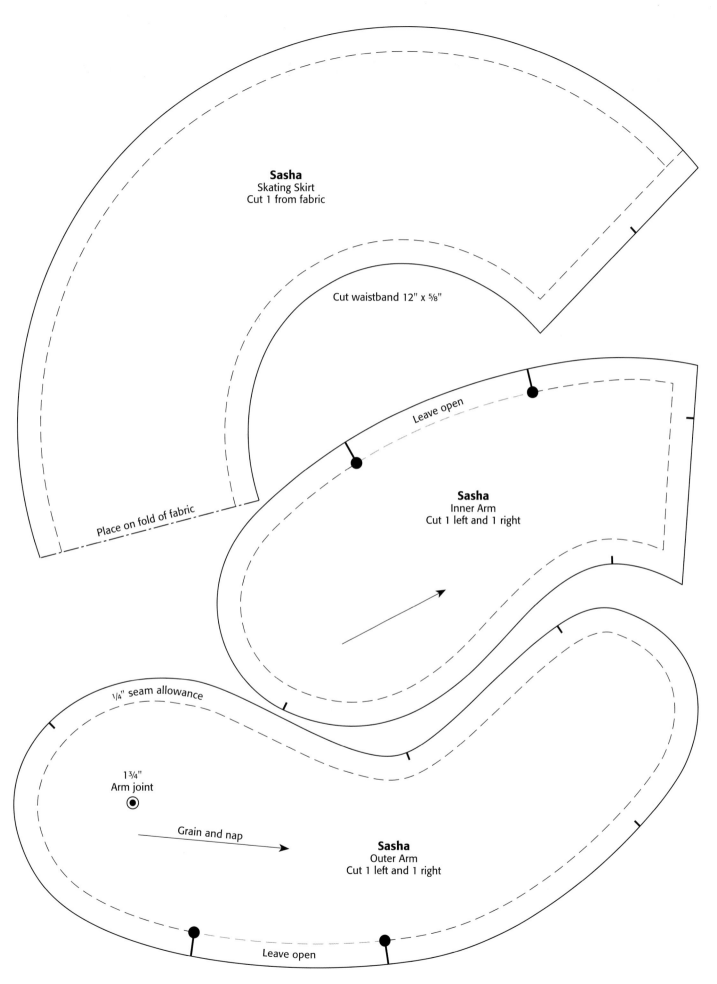

**Sasha**
Skating Skirt
Cut 1 from fabric

Cut waistband 12" x ⅝"

Place on fold of fabric

Leave open

**Sasha**
Inner Arm
Cut 1 left and 1 right

¼" seam allowance

1¾"
Arm joint

Grain and nap

**Sasha**
Outer Arm
Cut 1 left and 1 right

Leave open

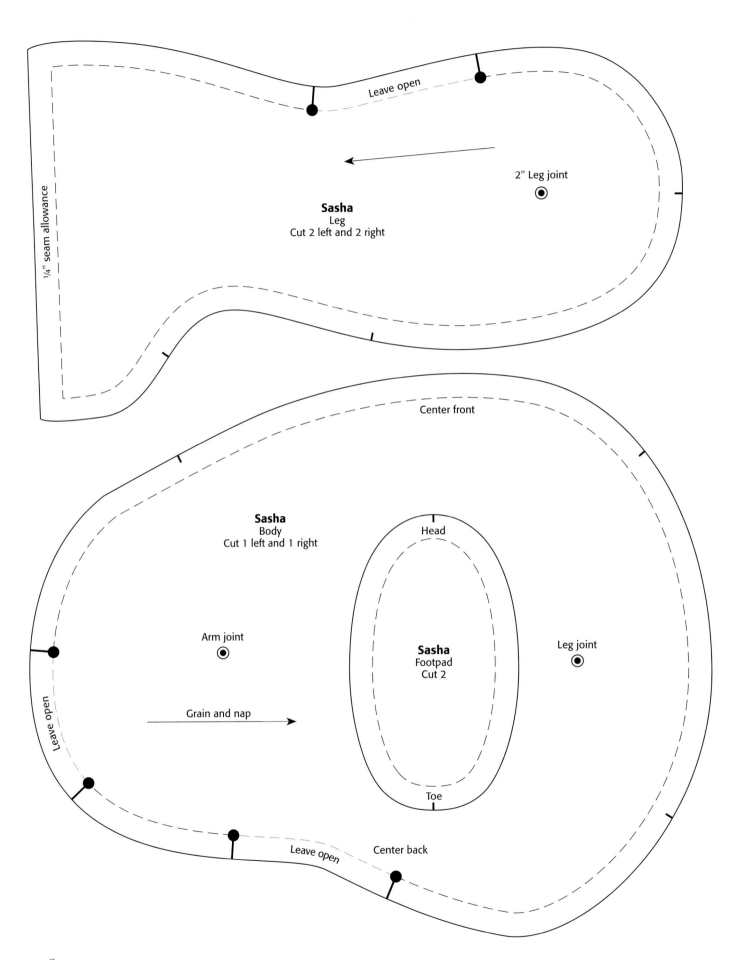

Leave open

¹⁄₄" seam allowance

**Sasha**
Leg
Cut 2 left and 2 right

2" Leg joint

Center front

**Sasha**
Body
Cut 1 left and 1 right

Arm joint

Leg joint

Head

**Sasha**
Footpad
Cut 2

Grain and nap

Leave open

Toe

Leave open

Center back

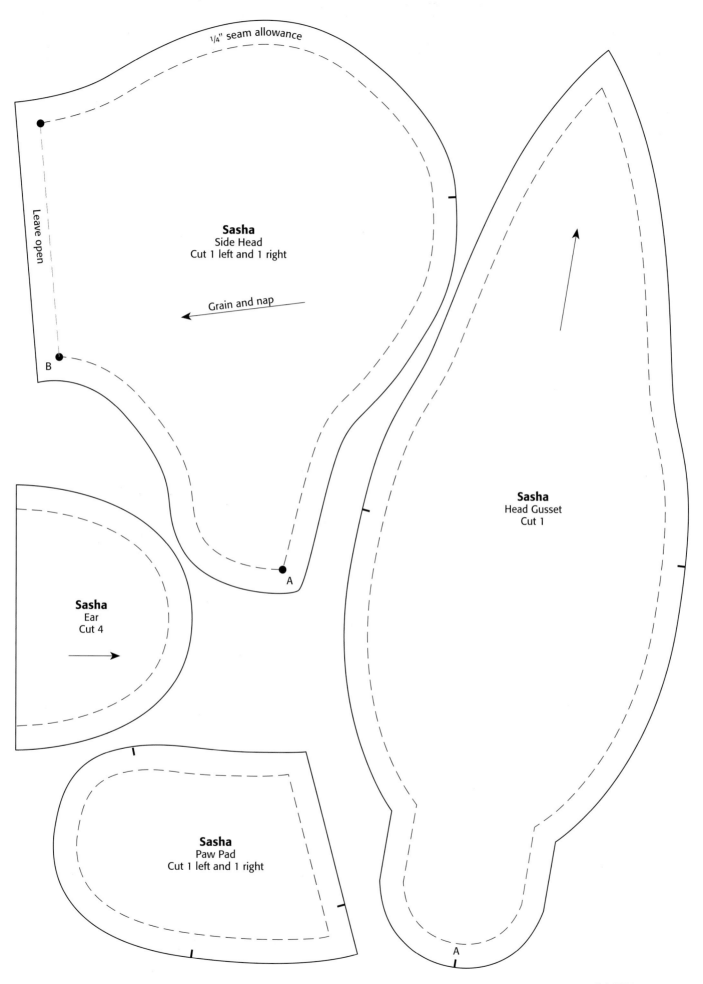

¼" seam allowance

Leave open

**Sasha**
Side Head
Cut 1 left and 1 right

Grain and nap

B

A

**Sasha**
Ear
Cut 4

**Sasha**
Head Gusset
Cut 1

**Sasha**
Paw Pad
Cut 1 left and 1 right

¼" seam allowance

A

# MISSY

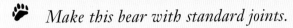   Make this bear with standard joints.

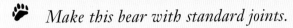 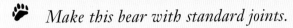   Make a bear with Jiggle Joints.

     Try fabric painting on mohair.

BEAR FACTS: BOTH ANTIQUE AND MODERN BEARS ARE ON DISPLAY AT THE TEDDY BEAR MUSEUM LOCATED IN NAPLES, FLORIDA. OTHER MUSEUMS ARE IN ENGLAND, JAPAN, AND THE STEIFF FACTORY IN GERMANY.

*14" Jointed Bear (unpainted and painted) by Linda Mead, 1998, Spare Bear Parts, Interlochen, Michigan*

# MATERIALS

* ¼ yd. 5/8"-long string mohair fabric
* 3" x 7" suede cloth for paw pads and foot pads
* Size 5 perle cotton for nose and mouth
* 1 pair of 9 mm amber glass eyes with pupils or 1 pair 15 mm black glass eyes
* Firm-pack stuffing or plastic pellets
* Cotter-pin joints for beginning bear maker
  * Ten 1¾" joint disks
  * 10 cotter-pin washers
  * Five 2" cotter pins
* Optional
  * Jiggle Joints for intermediate bear maker
    * Ten 1¾" disks
    * 20 cotter-pin washers
    * Ten 1½" cotter pins
  * Clear nail polish or varnish for nose
  * 12 colors of Dye-na-Flow paints
  * Airbrush

# DIRECTIONS

*All seam allowances are ¼".*

Refer to "Getting Started" on pages 21–24 for making patterns, cutting fabric, and transferring markings.

**GROOMING SEAMS:** After sewing each seam, pull fur out of seams on both wrong and right sides.

**ARMS:** Pin and sew paw pad to inner arm at wrist edge, matching A marks. Fold arm right sides together, match marks, and pin. Sew around arm, leaving an opening as marked. Repeat for other arm.

**LEGS:** Fold leg right sides together, match marks, and pin. Starting at toe, sew around leg. Leave an opening on side as marked and an opening at the bottom for foot pad. Then match and pin toe mark on foot pad to toe seam of leg. Match and pin heel mark on foot pad to heel mark on leg. Pin foot pad to each side of leg. Place additional pins between these 4 pins as needed to keep raw edges of foot pad and leg even and the fullness equally distributed. With foot pad on top, sew around foot. Refer to "Foot Pads" on page 28. Repeat for other leg.

**BODY:** Pin 1 front and 1 back piece together at side seam, matching marks. Sew from neck edge to bottom corner. Repeat with remaining front and back pieces. Pin body halves together, matching all marks. Sew from upper

back "Leave open" mark and around hump. Skip a stitch at neck joint mark; then continue down front and around bottom to "Leave open" mark on lower back.

**HEAD WITH TRIANGLE MUZZLE** (page 29): If you want the fabric backing to show on the muzzle, pluck the fur from the seam allowance with tweezers before sewing. Pin head gusset to a side head piece, matching all marks. With gusset on top, sew from nose (B) to end of gusset. Repeat for other side head piece, leaving an opening as marked. Finish seam from end of gusset to neck edge, if necessary.

Sew darts in neck. Then pin side head pieces together along neck and sew from B, down chin and across neck, skipping one stitch at neck joint mark. Use contrasting thread for tailor tacks to mark ear and eye placements on outside of head.

**EARS:** Pin and sew 2 ear pieces together along curved edges, leaving straight edges open. Repeat for other ear.

**JOINTING AND STUFFING:** Attach head and limbs to body, referring to "Cotter-Pin Joints" on pages 46–47 or "Jiggle Joints" on page 47. Stuff head with firm-pack stuffing. Stuff body and limbs with polyester stuffing or a combination of polyester and plastic pellets and close openings.

**PAINTING**: *If you prefer not to paint your bear, skip this section and go directly to "Face" section below.*

I airbrushed 12 colors of Dye-na-Flow paints onto the bear in the photo. An airbrush uses compressed air to force a very small amount of paint to cover a large area. With a little practice, you can also achieve the same effect if you use a very small amount of paint on a paintbrush. To heat-set the paint, use a hair dryer set on high on the bear for 3 or 4 minutes. Because of the amount of paint used with a paintbrush, heat-set the paint after adding each color. Experiment on fabric scraps before painting your finished bear.

When you are ready, begin to paint your bear, starting with about a 2" circle in one color. Randomly paint circles in the first color, leaving plenty of space to add additional colors. Heat set the first color. Then change colors and paint next to the first color. Overlapping two colors will make a third color. Overlapping too many colors may create a mottled brown. Pay special attention to painting between the joints to cover the white fur completely. Continue until the whole bear is covered. Be sure to finish the face last, after you have had some practice painting the rest of the bear. For an attention-getting face, use light colors around the eyes.

**FACE:** Referring to pages 35–44, install eyes, embroider nose and mouth, and attach ears.

**OPTIONAL:** Add clear fingernail polish or varnish to the nose to make it shiny (see page 41).

**FINISHING:** Groom the fur with a wire brush, especially at the seams. Tie a ribbon around neck, if desired. Give your new bear a hug!

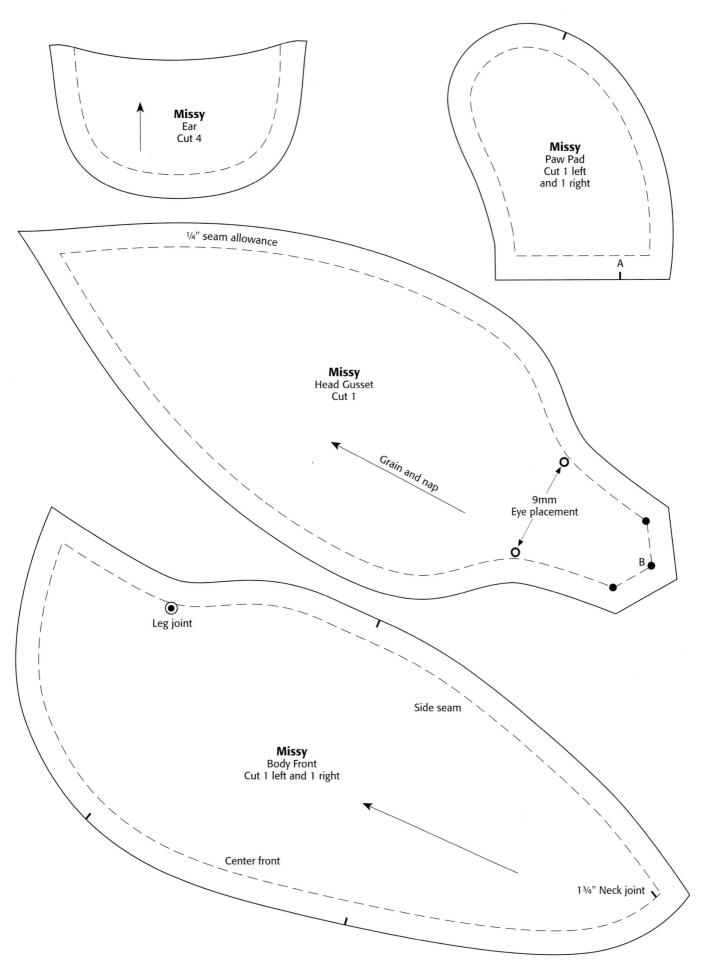

**Missy**
Ear
Cut 4

**Missy**
Paw Pad
Cut 1 left
and 1 right

A

¼" seam allowance

**Missy**
Head Gusset
Cut 1

Grain and nap

9mm
Eye placement

B

Leg joint

Side seam

**Missy**
Body Front
Cut 1 left and 1 right

Center front

1¾" Neck joint

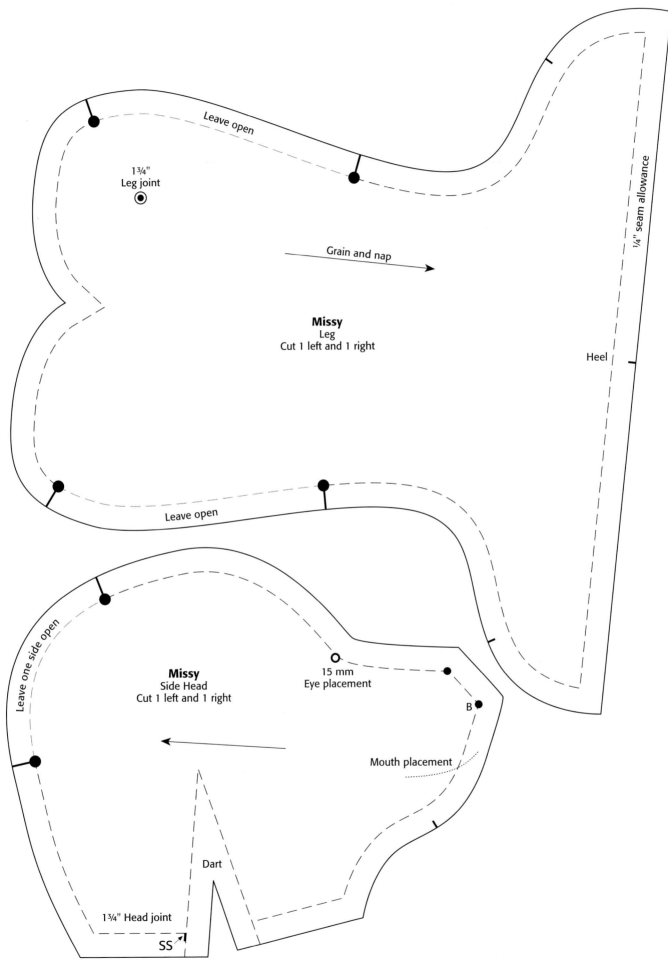

Leave open

1¾"
Leg joint

Grain and nap

**Missy**
Leg
Cut 1 left and 1 right

¼" seam allowance

Heel

Leave open

Leave one side open

**Missy**
Side Head
Cut 1 left and 1 right

15 mm
Eye placement

B

Mouth placement

Dart

1¾" Head joint

SS

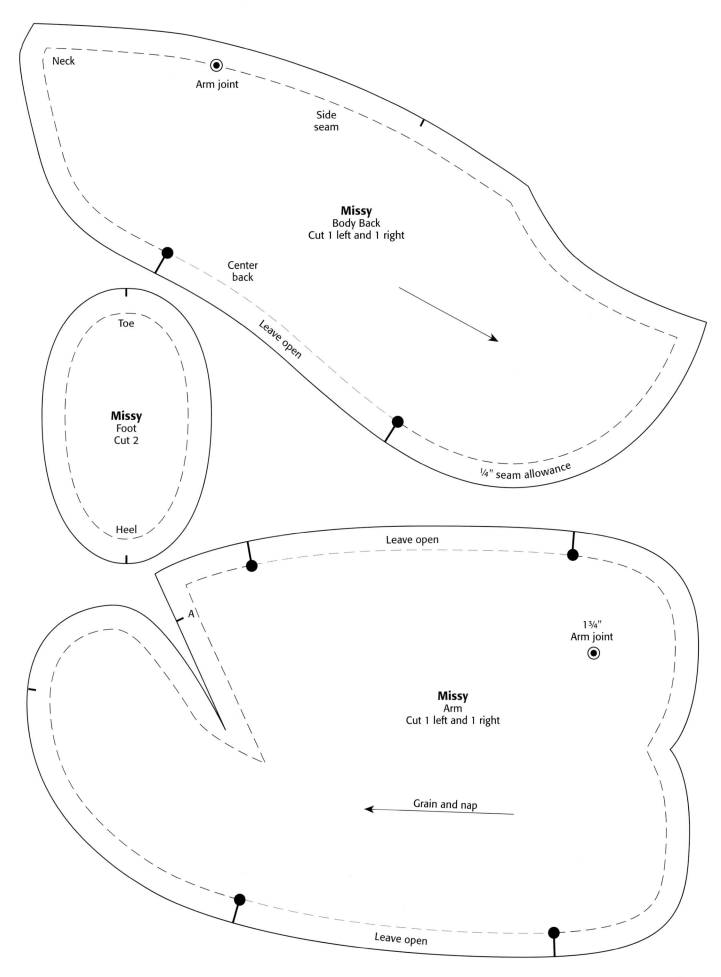

Neck

Arm joint

Side
seam

**Missy**
Body Back
Cut 1 left and 1 right

Center
back

Toe

**Missy**
Foot
Cut 2

Heel

Leave open

¼" seam allowance

Leave open

A

1¾"
Arm joint

**Missy**
Arm
Cut 1 left and 1 right

Grain and nap

Leave open

# AMBROSE

🐾 🐾 *Create this wonderful polar bear that has 12 joints to give him almost limitless poses.*

🐾 🐾 🐾 *The "Artist Tip" explains how to adapt patterns to reduce the bulk of long furs in a neck joint.*

BEAR FACTS: WHEN STANDING, AN ADULT POLAR BEAR IS ABOUT 10' TALL AND WEIGHS OVER 1,000 POUNDS. POLAR BEAR PAWS ARE ABOUT 12" WIDE. DESPITE THEIR SIZE, POLAR BEARS ARE OFTEN VERY PLAYFUL AND ENJOY AMUSING THEMSELVES BY ROLLING IN THE SNOW AND SLIDING DOWN A HILL. A POLAR BEAR'S FUR IS ACTUALLY CLEAR. IT APPEARS A YELLOWISH WHITE AS LIGHT IS REFLECTED ON IT. THE UNDERLYING SKIN IS BLACK.

*23" Bear with 12 Joints by JoAn Brown, 1999, Brown Bear Co., Blaine, Minnesota*

# MATERIALS

* ½ yd. of ¾" string mohair fur fabric
* 8" x 11" square wool felt or Ultrasuede for paw pads and foot pads
* 1 pair of 14 mm black eyes
* 4" x 60" (or an equivalent amount) lightweight canvas or other very strong fabric for size #1 and #2 circles
* Locknut and bolt joints
  * Eight 2" disks for paws and arms
  * Sixteen 3" disks for head, neck, legs, and feet
  * 12 bolts
  * 12 locknuts

# DIRECTIONS

*All seam allowances are ¼".*

Refer to "Getting Started" on pages 21–24 for making patterns, cutting fabric, and transferring markings. Refer to the pattern layout on page 89 before cutting pieces.

**GROOMING SEAMS:** After stitching, pull fur out of seams on both the wrong and right sides.

**CANVAS CIRCLES TO REDUCE BULK:** From lightweight canvas, cut out 4 size #1 circles and 12 size #2 circles. Mark the center of each circle and cut a small hole for the joint hardware. Then sew the circles to the bear sections, which is easy to do. With the wrong side of the section facing out, place the circle inside the section so that it will be sewn to the right side of the fur. Sewing canvas circles in the bear parts is similar to sewing a foot pad in a leg. Clip seam allowances on fur as necessary for a good fit. When you turn the section right side out, there is a nice, clean edge where the circle is sewn to the fur. This edge will be hidden when the sections are jointed.

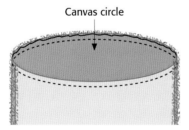

Canvas circle

**HEAD WITH ROUNDED MUZZLE** (page 30): Sew dart on each side head piece. Match and pin side head pieces along chin, and sew from A to B. Pin head gusset to a side head piece, matching all marks. With gusset on top, sew from nose (A) to end of gusset (C). Repeat with other side head piece, leaving an opening as marked. Sew a size #2 circle in neck edge of

## ARTIST TIP

Longer furs can create bulk in the neck seam. To reduce the bulk, sew circles of strong fabric in place of the fur between the joint disks.

To do this on your own patterns, remove the fabric from both the head and body that would normally be between the disks. Remove the amount of half the measurement of the joint disk. For example, if the diameter of the disk is 2", cut 1" from the neck edges. Cut 2 fabric circles that are the same size as the disks. Sew the circles in the neck opening with a ¼" seam allowance. Assemble the joint as usual, passing the hardware through a hole in the center of the circles.

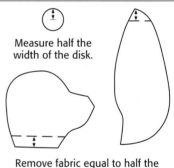

Measure half the width of the disk.

Remove fabric equal to half the measurement of the joint disk.

## ABOUT THE PATTERN

Ambrose was designed by JoAn Brown, a Spare Bear Parts Certified Instructor. This unique multi-joint pattern allows you to change the tilt of his head so that he can stand on all 4 feet or sit up and look straight ahead. The neck is a separate section that is wider on one side than the other. Turning the neck section will move the head up or down. The extra joints in the limbs add to his range of motion.

Turn Ambrose's neck section to tilt his head up or down.

head. Use contrasting thread for tailor tacks to mark ear and eye placements on outside of head.

**NECK:** Pin neck pieces together, matching all marks. Sew short side together from D to E. Sew long side together from F to G, leaving an opening as marked. Sew 2 size #2 circles in the top and bottom of the neck.

**BODY:** Pin body front pieces together at the center front, matching all marks. Sew from neck (H) to bottom (I). Pin body back pieces together at the center back, matching all marks. Sew from neck (J) to bottom (K), leaving an opening as marked. Pin body halves together, matching marks. Sew from neck to K/I at bottom on both sides. Leave neck open. Sew a size #2 circle in the body along the neck edge. Make small holes for arm and leg joints.

**ANKLES:** Pin 2 ankle pieces together, matching all marks. Sew short sides together from L to M. Sew long sides together from N to O, leaving an opening as marked. Sew 2 size # 2 circles in the top and bottom of ankle. Repeat for other ankle.

**FEET:** Pin 2 foot pieces together, matching all marks. Sew curved sides together from P to Q. Sew opposite sides together from R to S, leaving an opening as marked. Sew a size #2 circle in top of foot. On bottom of foot, match and pin toe mark on foot pad to toe seam of foot. Then match and pin heel mark on foot pad to heel seam on foot. Pin foot pad to each side of leg. Place additional pins between these 4 pins as needed to keep raw edges of foot pad and foot even and the fullness equally distributed. With the foot pad on top, sew around foot. Refer to "Foot Pads" on page 28. Repeat for other foot.

**UPPER LEGS:** Pin 2 upper leg pieces together, matching all marks. Sew all around curve from T to U, leaving an opening as marked. Sew a size #2 circle in bottom of upper leg. Make a small hole for joint on inside of leg. Repeat for other upper leg.

**PAWS:** Pin mohair paw to felt paw, matching marks. Sew all around curve from V to W, leaving an opening as marked. Sew a size #1 circle in top of paw. Repeat for other paw.

**ARMS:** Pin 2 arm pieces together, matching all marks. Sew all around curve from X to Y, leaving an opening as marked. Sew a size #1 circle in bottom of arm. Make a small hole for joint on inside of arm. Repeat for other arm.

**EARS AND TAIL:** Pin and sew 2 ear pieces together along curved edges, leaving straight edges open. Repeat for other ear and tail.

**JOINTING:** When you have the 13 sections of the bear sewn, turn them all right side out and arrange them on a table in the order that they will be sewn together. Check to make sure left and right sections are placed appropriately. Joint the sections, referring to "Locknut and Bolt (or Tap-Bolt) Joints" on pages 47–48. Use 2" disks for paw and arm joints and 3" disks for all other joints. Tighten each joint until it can be moved only with force. If you insert the bolt toward the larger of the 2 sections being jointed, you will have extra space for tightening the nut.

STUFFING: Firmly stuff each section with firm-pack polyester, and close openings. Add plastic pellets to the polyester stuffing in the body if you want to add weight.

FACE: Referring to pages 35–44, install eyes, embroider nose and mouth, and attach ears.

TAIL: Place a little stuffing in tail and stitch in place with a ladder stitch.

FINISHING: Groom bear with a wire brush, especially at the seams. Give your new bear a big hug!

A turn of the neck changes the angle to allow Ambrose to stand on all four feet.

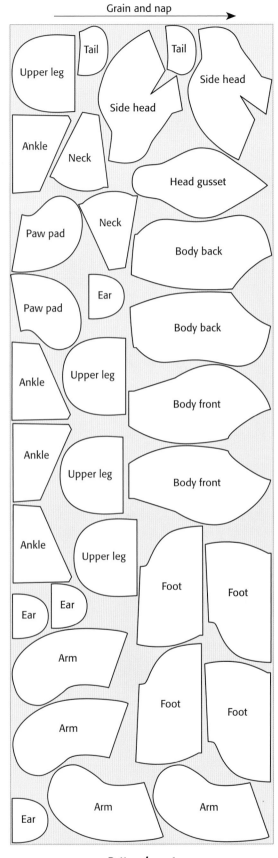

**Pattern layout**

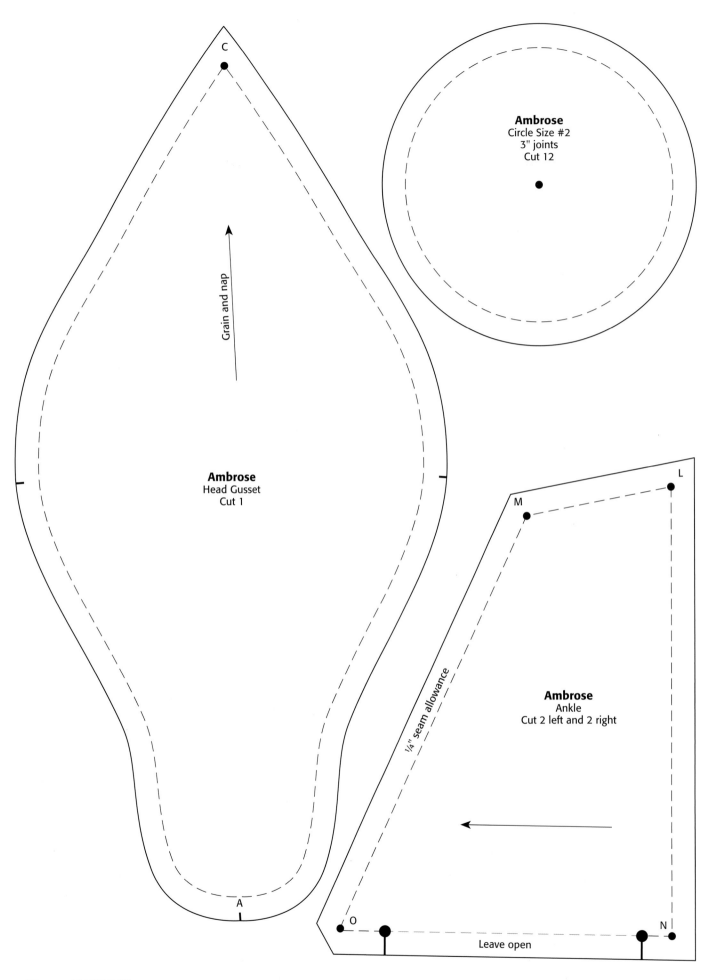

**Ambrose**
Circle Size #2
3" joints
Cut 12

C

Grain and nap

**Ambrose**
Head Gusset
Cut 1

A

¼" seam allowance

L

M

**Ambrose**
Ankle
Cut 2 left and 2 right

O

N

Leave open

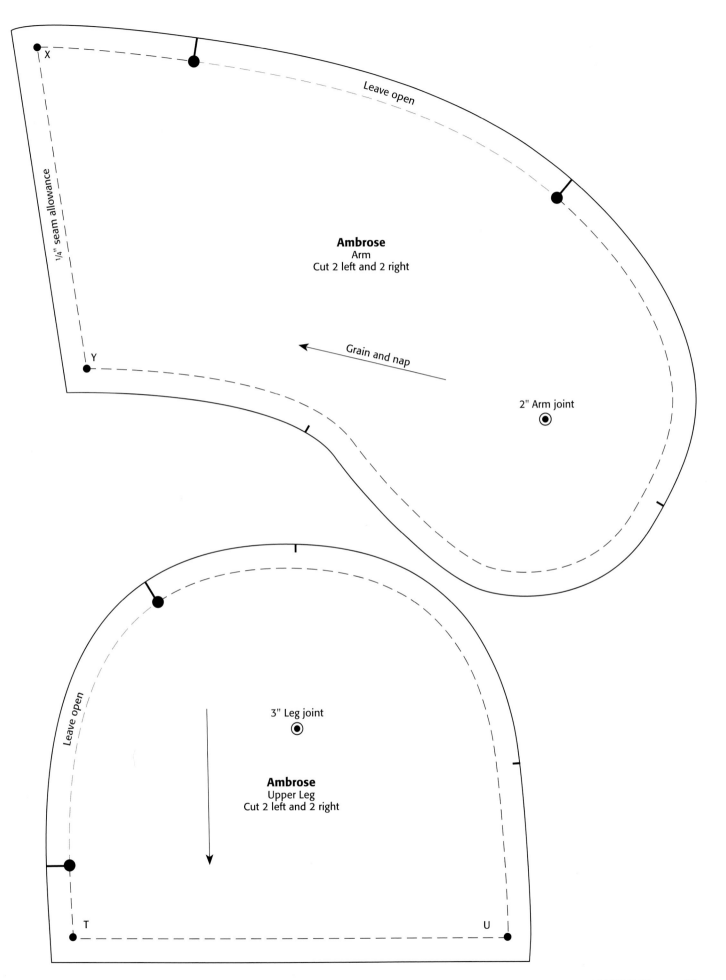

X

1/4" seam allowance

Leave open

**Ambrose**
Arm
Cut 2 left and 2 right

Y

Grain and nap

2" Arm joint

Leave open

3" Leg joint

**Ambrose**
Upper Leg
Cut 2 left and 2 right

T

U

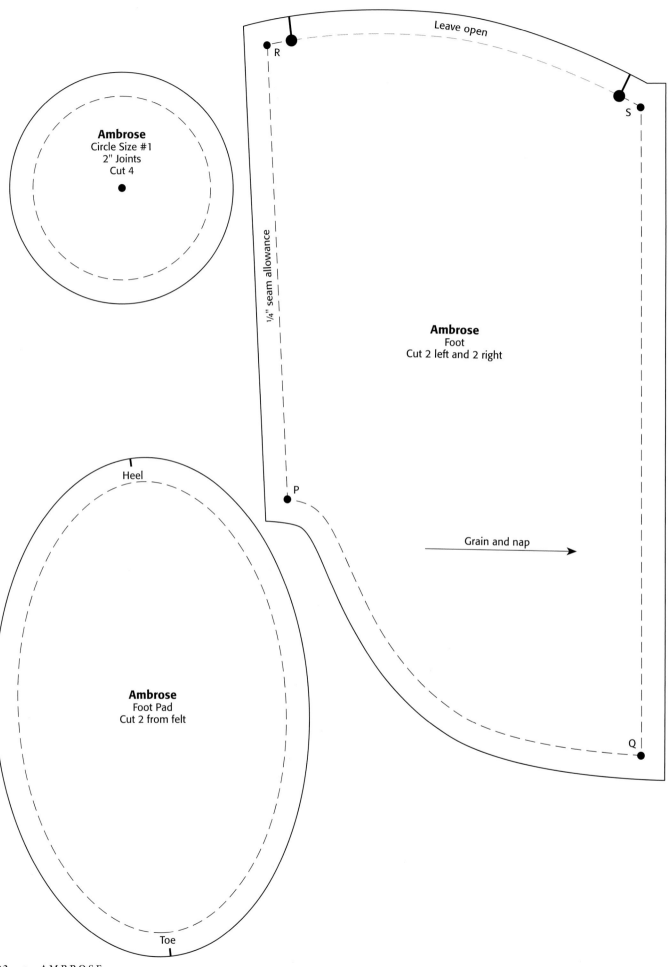

**Ambrose**
Circle Size #1
2" Joints
Cut 4

**Ambrose**
Foot
Cut 2 left and 2 right

Leave open

R

S

¼" seam allowance

P

Grain and nap

Q

Heel

**Ambrose**
Foot Pad
Cut 2 from felt

Toe

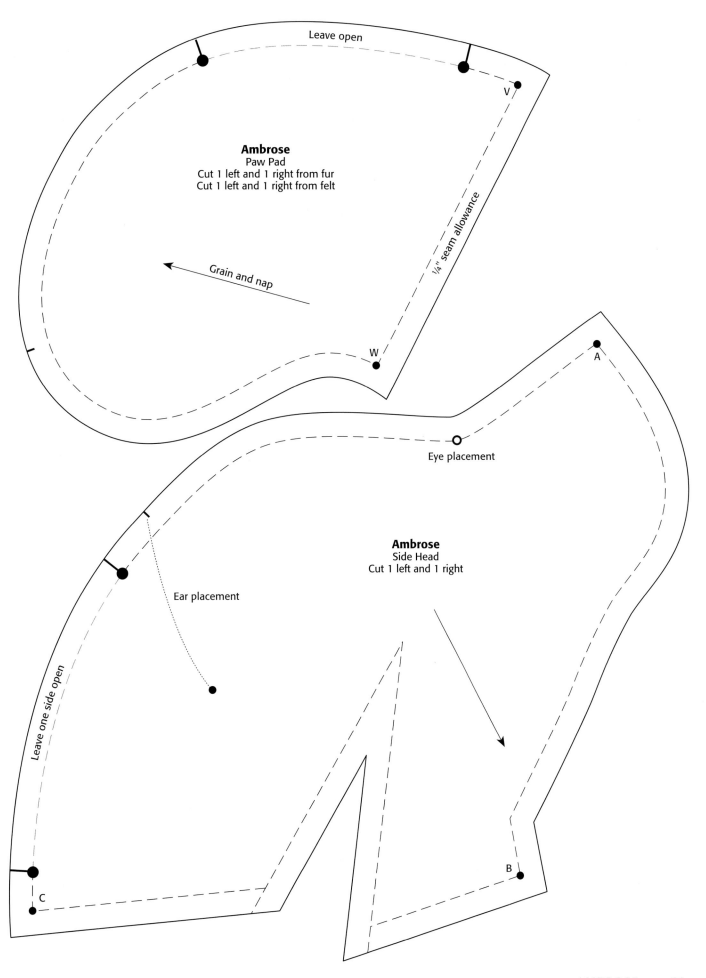

**Ambrose**
Paw Pad
Cut 1 left and 1 right from fur
Cut 1 left and 1 right from felt

Leave open

V

¼" seam allowance

Grain and nap

W

A

Eye placement

**Ambrose**
Side Head
Cut 1 left and 1 right

Ear placement

Leave one side open

B

C

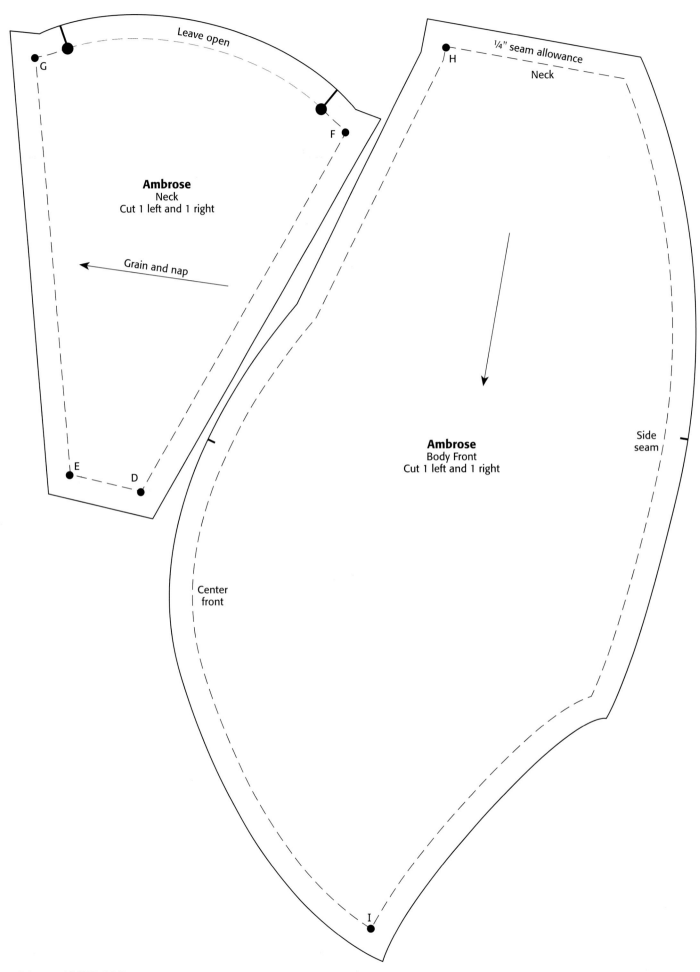

Leave open

G

**Ambrose**
Neck
Cut 1 left and 1 right

Grain and nap

E          D

F

H          ¼" seam allowance

Neck

**Ambrose**
Body Front
Cut 1 left and 1 right

Side
seam

Center
front

I

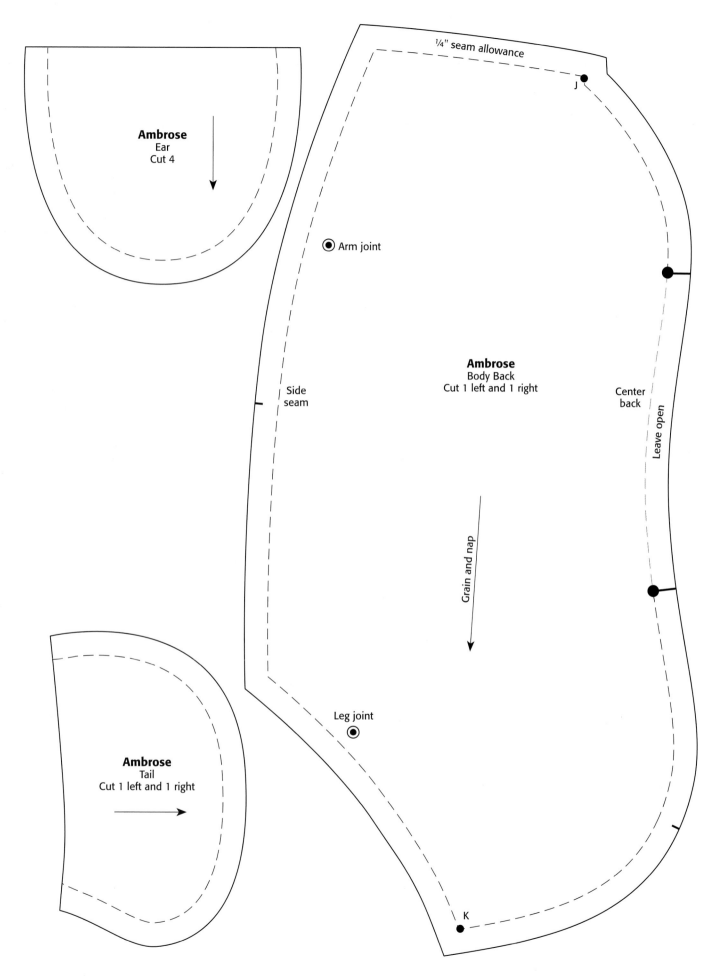

**Ambrose**
Ear
Cut 4

¼" seam allowance

J

● Arm joint

Side
seam

**Ambrose**
Body Back
Cut 1 left and 1 right

Center
back

Leave open

Grain and nap

Leg joint

**Ambrose**
Tail
Cut 1 left and 1 right

K

¼" seam allowance

# RED BEAR

 *This bear is easy to hand or machine sew.*

  *Learn to install a hidden needle holder.*

---

BEAR FACTS: MANY SMALL BEARS IN THE EARLY 1900S WERE UNIQUELY DESIGNED TO HOLD PERFUME BOTTLES, LIPSTICK, COIN PURSES, COMPACTS, AND MIRRORS. BRIGHT COLORS WERE FAVORITES OF THE SCHUCO MINIATURE BEAR LINE.

*5 ½" Jointed Bear with Optional Needle Holder by Linda Mead, 1999, Spare Bear Parts, Interlochen, Michigan*

# MATERIALS

* 12" square of 3/16"-pile mohair fur fabric
* 1 pair of 4 mm onyx beads for eyes
* Size 8 perle cotton for nose and mouth
* Kapok or firm-pack polyester stuffing
* Cotter-pin joints
  * Ten ½" disks
  * 10 cotter-pin washers
  * Five ¾" cotter pins

NOTE: *If you insert the wooden needle holder, you will only need 4 joint sets.*

* Optional
  * Small, wooden needle holder
  * Water-based fabric glue

# DIRECTIONS

*All seam allowances are ⅛".*

Refer to "Getting Started" on pages 21–24 for making patterns, cutting fabric, and transferring markings. Refer to the pattern layout on page 99 before cutting pieces.

**GROOMING SEAMS:** After sewing each seam, pull fur out of seams on both wrong and right sides.

**ARMS:** Fold arm piece right sides together, match marks, and pin. Hand sew around arm, leaving an opening as marked. Repeat for other arm.

**LEGS:** Fold leg piece right sides together, match marks, and pin. Hand sew around leg, leaving an opening as marked. Repeat for other leg.

**BODY:** Pin and hand sew dart at hip. Pin front and back body halves together, matching marks. Starting at front neck edge, hand sew around body, leaving an opening as marked. Leave neck edge open.
  * For needle holder, see "Optional Needle Holder" on page 98.
  * For jointed neck, see "Stuffing and Jointing" on page 98.

**HEAD WITH TRIANGLE MUZZLE** (page 29): To trim muzzle like the bear in the photograph, pluck fur from muzzle and seam area with tweezers before stitching head together. Use Fray Check or Stop Fraying on backing before removing fur. Refer to "Trimming the Muzzle Fur" on page 39.

Pin head gusset to a side head piece, matching all marks. With gusset on top, hand sew from nose (A) to end of gusset. Repeat for other side head piece. Finish seam from end of gusset to neck edge. Pin side head pieces together at chin seam, matching all marks. Hand sew from nose (A), down chin to neck edge. Leave the neck open.

## ARTIST REMINDER

To prevent raveling of the coarse woven backing, use Fray Check or Stop Fraying. If tracing the pattern to the fabric, be sure to cut away any ink because these glues can cause even permanent ink to run.

## ABOUT THE PATTERN

The neck/shoulder area of Red Bear was designed to snuggly fit a common wooden needle holder, but you could substitute the needle holder with other containers. You want to make sure the container will fit inside the bear. Before cutting the fabric for the body, measure the length and width of the body (without seam allowances) and compare it to the length and width of the needle holder, perfume bottle, or other container.

Use contrasting thread for tailor tacks to mark ear and eye placements on outside of head.

**EARS:** Pin and hand sew 2 ear pieces together along curved edges, leaving straight edges open. Repeat for other ear.

**STUFFING AND JOINTING:** You may use cotter-pin joints or thread joints (see pages 52–53). See below for installing needle holder instead of standard neck joint. For cotter-pin neck joint, stuff head firmly to within ⅜" of neck edge, making sure to hard pack the muzzle. Place cotter-pin assembly in neck, and use a spider web stitch (see page 52) to gather neck edge of head. Use a long running stitch to gather the neck edge of the body. Place cotter pin from head in center of gathers at body neck edge. Complete joint. Attach limbs, referring to "Cotter-Pin Joints" on pages 46–47. Stuff limbs and body, and close opening.

**FACE:** Referring to pages 35–44, install eyes, embroider nose and mouth, and attach ears.

**OPTIONAL NEEDLE HOLDER:** Attach limbs to body with cotter pins before installing the needle holder. You may need to flatten the cotter pins to allow the needle holder to fit. Stuff head but not the neck area. Trim fur ¼" from neck edge of head. Fold trimmed fabric into neck. Use a double strand of thread to sew a running stitch along folded neck edge. Do not gather threads yet.

Put needle-holder cap into neck to be sure that there is enough room in the head for the cap to fit properly. Make adjustments, adding or removing stuffing as necessary. Apply a thin bead of glue around side edges of the cap and slide cap in position. When cap is in position, with the folded fabric edge aligned with the bottom of cap, gather threads tight and tie off. Allow glue to dry before burying threads.

Trim fur ¼" from neck edge of body. Fold trimmed fabric into body. Use a double strand of thread to sew a running stitch along the folded body edge. Do not gather threads yet.

Place needle holder into body through neck opening to test size. Apply a thin bead of glue to the needle holder just below the area covered by the cap. Do not allow glue to run onto area that will fit into cap. Slide holder into body, lining up the folded fabric edge with the shoulder of needle holder—not the area that fits into cap. Gather threads tight and tie off. Allow glue to dry before burying threads. Stuff body through back opening and close opening.

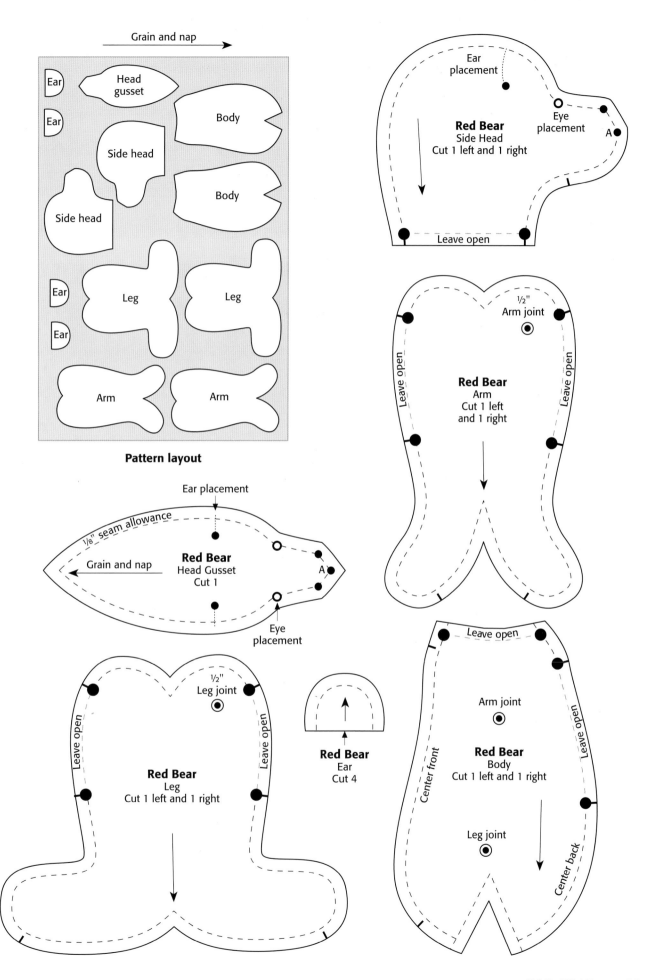

**Grain and nap** →

Ear

Ear

Head gusset

Body

Side head

Body

Side head

Ear

Leg

Leg

Ear

Arm

Arm

**Pattern layout**

Ear placement

**Red Bear**
Side Head
Cut 1 left and 1 right

Eye placement

A

Leave open

½"
Arm joint

Leave open

Leave open

**Red Bear**
Arm
Cut 1 left
and 1 right

Ear placement

⅛" seam allowance

Grain and nap ←

**Red Bear**
Head Gusset
Cut 1

A

Eye placement

½"
Leg joint

Leave open

Leave open

**Red Bear**
Leg
Cut 1 left and 1 right

**Red Bear**
Ear
Cut 4

Leave open

Arm joint

Center front

Leave open

**Red Bear**
Body
Cut 1 left and 1 right

Leg joint

Center back

RED BEAR • 99

# BABY BEAR

 *Make an easy jointed bear with fabric nose and tilted head.*

BEAR FACTS: MOST FEMALE BEARS HAVE TWIN CUBS BUT THREE OR FOUR CUBS ARE NOT UNUSUAL. MOTHER BEARS RAISE THEIR YOUNG WITHOUT THE FATHERS. THEY ARE VERY PROTECTIVE OF THEIR YOUNG BECAUSE THE MORE AGGRESSIVE MALES SOMETIMES ATTEMPT TO KILL THE CUBS. BY AGE THREE, MOST CUBS LEAVE THEIR MOTHERS TO LIVE ON THEIR OWN.

*11" Jointed Bear with Velvet Nose by Linda Mead, 1999, Spare Bear Parts, Interlochen, Michigan*

# MATERIALS

* ★ ¼ yd. of ½" straight pile mohair fur fabric for both bears
* ★ 3" x 7" piece of suede cloth for paw pads and foot pads
* ★ 2" square of brown upholstery velvet for nose
* ★ Size 3 perle cotton for mouth
* ★ 1 pair of 10 mm amber glass eyes with pupils
* ★ Excelsior to stuff muzzle
* ★ Firm-pack polyester stuffing
* ★ Rivet joints
    * • One 1½" joint disk for head
    * • Nine 1¼" joint disks for arms, legs, and body/neck
    * • 10 rivet washers
    * • 5 rivets

# DIRECTIONS

*All seam allowances are ¼".*

Refer to "Getting Started" on pages 21–24 for making patterns, cutting fabric, and transferring markings.

**GROOMING SEAMS:** After sewing each seam, pull fur out of seams on both wrong and right sides. Take extra care to groom the seams when working on straight furs. Seams are much more evident on straight fur than curly fur.

**ARMS:** Pin paw pad to inner arm at wrist edge, matching A marks. Fold arm right sides together, match marks, and pin. Sew around arm, leaving an opening as marked. Repeat for other arm.

**LEGS:** Pin 2 leg pieces together, matching all marks. Starting at toe, sew around leg, leaving an opening as marked and at bottom for foot pad. Match and pin toe mark on foot pad to toe seam of leg. Then match and pin heel mark on foot pad to heel seam on leg. Pin foot pad to each side of leg. Place additional pins between these 4 pins as needed to keep raw edges of foot pad and leg even and the fullness equally distributed. With the foot pad on top, sew around foot. Refer to "Foot Pads" on page 28. Repeat with other leg.

**BODY:** Pin 1 front and 1 back piece together at side seam, matching all marks. Sew from neck edge to bottom corner. Repeat with remaining front and back pieces. Pin body halves together, matching all marks. Starting at "Leave open" mark on upper back, sew around hump, down front, and around bottom to "Leave open" mark on lower back.

**HEAD WITH SQUARE MUZZLE** (page 30): Pin side head pieces together, matching B marks. Sew from nose (B), down chin and across

Moving the neck joint placement offers a variety of possible poses that convey a mood or activity, including shy (chin down), curious (head tilted to side), proud (chin up), holding a violin (extreme tilt), or watching a balloon above (extreme chin up). These are just a few of the changes you can create by moving the neck joint.

**ABOUT THE PATTERN**

The pattern for Baby Bear is a smaller version of a larger, adult-bear pattern. After reducing the head, I also decreased the muzzle length and increased the width of the head gusset because bear cubs have small noses and large foreheads when compared to adult bears.

neck, skipping one stitch just forward of neck center at mark. This will be the opening for the joint hardware. Continue sewing to back of head. Pin center of head gusset (B) to chin seam. Sew across nose between 2 corner notches, pivot, and realign side head edges. Beginning at center (B), stitch to other corner, pivot, and sew other side head piece, leaving an opening as marked. Finish seam from end of gusset to neck edge. Use contrasting thread for tailor tacks to mark ear and eye placements on outside of head.

EARS: Pin and sew 2 ear pieces together along curved edges, leaving straight edges open. Repeat for other ear.

JOINTING AND STUFFING: Make holes at joint marks for arms and legs. For the neck joint, cut a hole ¼" to side of seam on front body. This will result in a tilted head. Use a large disk in the head and a smaller disk in the neck. The difference in the disk sizes will help create a wide face.

Attach limbs and head to body, referring to "Rivet Joints" on pages 49–50. Stuff muzzle with excelsior. Use firm-pack polyester stuffing for the rest of the head and for the limbs.

FACE: Referring to pages 35–44, install eyes, trim muzzle, make fabric nose, embroider mouth, and attach ears.

FINISHING: Brush and steam the mohair fur to smooth out the seams. Give your new bear a big hug!

# BABY BEAR'S HAT AND DRESS

## MATERIALS
- ★ 2 yds. of cotton eyelet trim, 7" to 8" wide
- ★ 1 yd. of ⅛"-wide ribbon
- ★ 3 yds. of ⅜"-wide picot ribbon
- ★ 1¼ yds. of 4"-wide flat lace
- ★ 3 baby buttons
- ★ 1 small snap (size 4/0)

## HAT DIRECTIONS

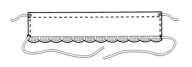

Fig. 75

1. Cut one 12½" piece of 7"-wide trim. Measuring from the unfinished edge of the trim, cut 2½" off the trim. Hem the two short sides. Fold the cut edge underneath and sew a ⅜"-wide casing for ribbon.

2. Cut two 11" pieces of ⅛"-wide ribbon. Fold one end of ribbon under and sew to lower corner of finished cotton-eyelet trim edge so that ribbon hangs down. Sew second piece of ribbon to other corner. Cut 15" piece of ⅛"-wide ribbon and insert into casing. Leave a tail of ribbon at each end of casing. Holding both ribbon tails, push the fabric toward the center of the ribbon to gather it to form back of hat. Tie ends in a bow (see fig. 75).

# DRESS DIRECTIONS

The dress is constructed from the bottom up.

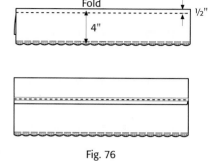

1. Cut 4 pieces from cotton eyelet trim: two 8"-long pieces, one 20½"-long piece, and one 24"-long piece.

2. On the 24"-long piece, fold unfinished edge of trim to wrong side so that remaining trim is 4" wide from finished edge. Sew ½" from the folded edge. Unfold the piece and sew the ⅜"-wide picot ribbon on top of the stitching line. Repeat with 20½" long piece (see fig. 76).

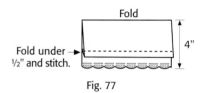

Fig. 76

3. Gather the 4"-wide flat lace to fit the 24" piece of cotton eyelet trim. Sew the gathered edge of the lace to the wrong side of the finished edge of the eyelet. Sew picot ribbon on top of stitching line.

4. Gather unfinished edge of 24" piece of cotton eyelet to fit 20½" piece of cotton eyelet. Sew the gathered edge to the wrong side of the finished edge of the 20½" piece. Sew the picot ribbon on top of stitching line.

Fig. 77

5. Fold the top unfinished edge of an 8"-long piece of cotton eyelet ½" to the wrong side. Then fold again to wrong side so that the remaining trim is 4" wide from finished edge. Sew through all 3 layers (see fig. 77). Sew picot ribbon on top of stitching line. Repeat for other 8" piece of eyelet. The finished edge of the eyelet trim will be the center front and center back of the bodice, and the folded edge will be the sleeve edge.

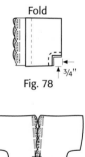

Fig. 78

6. To make side and underarm seams, fold bodice/sleeve in half with right sides together and cut edges aligned. Cut a ¾" square from folded sleeve edge and cut edges. Sew ¼" from the cut line, slightly rounding the seam around the cut corner. Clip into corner and turn to right side (see fig. 78). Repeat with second bodice/sleeve piece. Overlap front bodice pieces and tack together (see fig. 79).

Fig. 79

7. Gather top of skirt to fit bodice and pin, turning ¼" of skirt back seam over center back bodice on both ends for facing. Sew in place. Sew back seam of skirt to within 4" of waist. Hem remaining raw edges of skirt seam. Sew snap in place at waist.

8. Sew 3 small buttons at bodice front just above waist. Use remaining picot ribbon to tie a bow with long tails. Sew bow to center front waist.

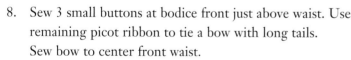

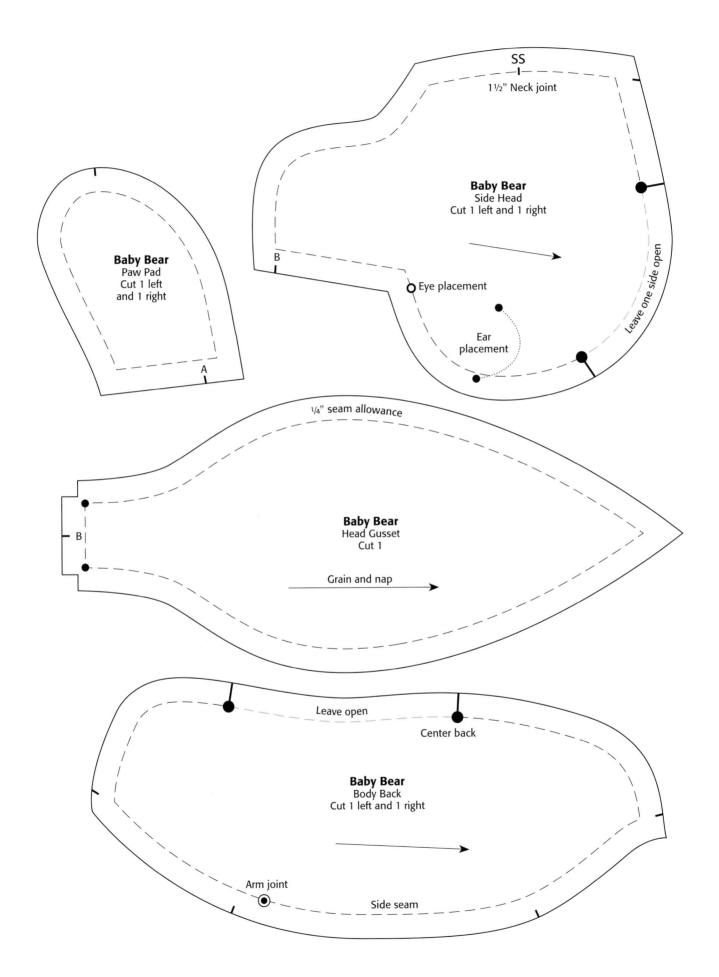

**Baby Bear**
Paw Pad
Cut 1 left
and 1 right

A

SS

1½" Neck joint

**Baby Bear**
Side Head
Cut 1 left and 1 right

B

Eye placement

Ear
placement

Leave one side open

¼" seam allowance

**Baby Bear**
Head Gusset
Cut 1

B

Grain and nap

Leave open

Center back

**Baby Bear**
Body Back
Cut 1 left and 1 right

Arm joint

Side seam

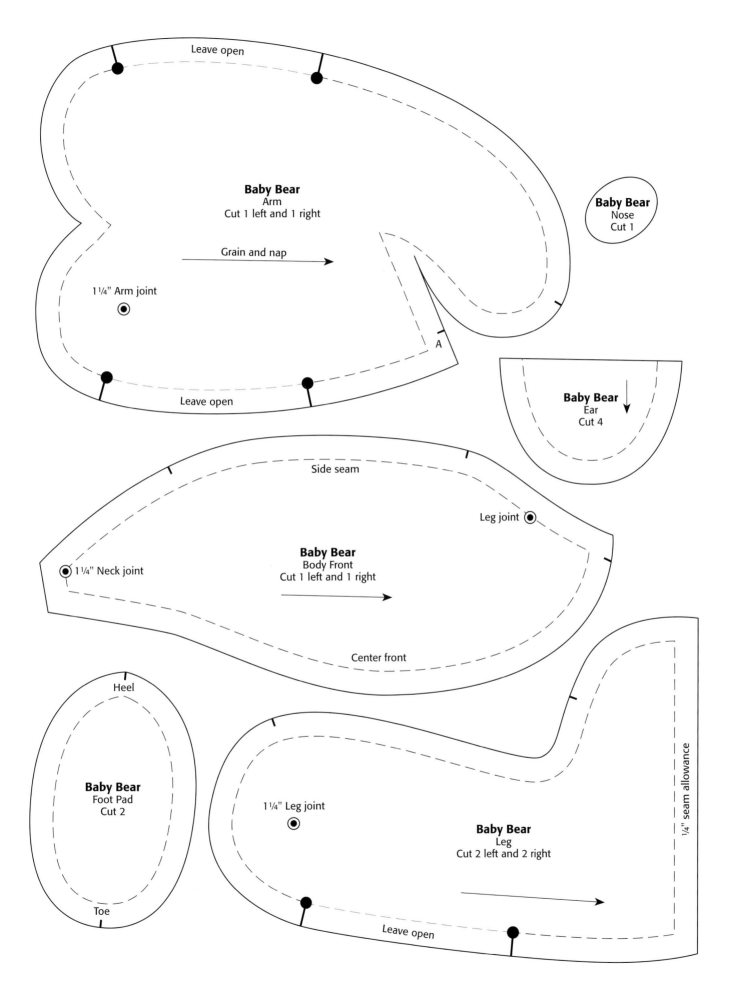

Leave open

**Baby Bear**
Arm
Cut 1 left and 1 right

Grain and nap

1¼" Arm joint

Leave open

A

**Baby Bear**
Nose
Cut 1

**Baby Bear**
Ear
Cut 4

Side seam

Leg joint

1¼" Neck joint

**Baby Bear**
Body Front
Cut 1 left and 1 right

Center front

Heel

**Baby Bear**
Foot Pad
Cut 2

Toe

1¼" Leg joint

**Baby Bear**
Leg
Cut 2 left and 2 right

Leave open

¼" seam allowance

# MEGAN ❧ *Try this easy-to-make bear and wardrobe.*

BEAR FACTS: IN 1982, TWENTY-FIVE THOUSAND ARCTOPHILES GATHERED AT THE PHILADELPHIA ZOO FOR THE FIRST AMERICAN TEDDY BEAR RALLY. *ARCTOPHILE* IS A TERM USED TO DESCRIBE A TEDDY BEAR COLLECTOR.

*9" Jointed Dress-up Bear by Linda Mead, 1999, Spare Bear Parts, Interlochen, Michigan*

# MATERIALS

* 6" x 54" of ³/₁₆"-pile mohair fur fabric
* 3" x 4" piece of felt for paw pads and foot pads
* 1 pair of 9 mm black glass eyes
* Size 3 perle cotton for nose and mouth
* Firm-pack polyester stuffing
* Cotter-pin joints
  * One 1¼" joint disk for head
  * Five 1" joint disks for legs and body
  * Four ¾" joint disks for arms
  * 10 cotter-pin washers
  * Five 1½" cotter pins

# DIRECTIONS

*All seam allowances are ⅛".*

Refer to "Getting Started" on pages 21–24 for making patterns, cutting fabric, and transferring markings.

**GROOMING SEAMS:** After sewing each seam, pull fur out of seams on both wrong and right sides.

**ARMS:** Pin and sew paw pad to inner arm at wrist edge, matching A marks. Pin inner and outer arms together, matching all marks. Sew around arm, leaving an opening as marked. Repeat for other arm.

**LEGS:** Fold leg right sides together and pin. Starting at the toe, sew around leg, leaving an opening as marked and at bottom for foot pad. Match and pin toe mark on foot pad to toe seam of leg. Then match and pin heel mark on foot pad to heel mark on leg. Pin foot pad to each side of leg. Place additional pins between these 4 pins as needed to keep the raw edges of the foot pad and leg even and the fullness equally distributed. With the foot pad facing up, hand sew around the foot. It is easier to hand sew foot pads on bears this small. Refer to "Foot Pads" on page 28. Repeat with other leg.

**BODY:** Pin and sew darts at top and bottom of body pieces. Pin body halves together, matching all marks. Starting at "Leave open" mark on upper back, sew around hump, down front, and around bottom to "Leave open" mark on lower back. Gather neck edge with a long running stitch.

**HEAD WITH BOX-CORNER MUZZLE** (page 29): Pin and sew darts on side head pieces. Pin head gusset to a side head piece, matching B marks. With gusset on top, sew from nose (B) to end of gusset. Repeat for other side head piece. Finish seam from end of gusset to neck edge. Fold muzzle (C) in half along center and sew from fold (C), down chin to neck.

## ARTIST REMINDER

Use short, black, glass-head pins or Try Eyes to find the right position for the eyes.

## ABOUT THE PATTERN

Megan was designed as a project to make with your special little girl. She is easy enough to make as a second or third sewing project to teach a child how to sew. Megan's straight body, long legs and short fur were designed to wear clothing. I hope you and your special little one have hours of enjoyment together making and dressing this bear. The clothing case is also a good project to do together. My granddaughter, Megan, helped me make the one shown on page 108 from a kit. See "Resources" on pages 152–153 for information on ordering the kit.

Refold the nose so that chin seam is lined up with center of the head gusset. Sew across nose to form a box-corner muzzle. Use contrasting thread for tailor tacks to mark ear and eye placements on outside of head.

EARS: Pin and sew 2 ear pieces together along curved edges, leaving straight edges open. Repeat for other ear.

JOINTING AND STUFFING: Make small holes at joint marks. For a tilted head, make hole for neck joint ¼" to side of front seam on body. Use 1¼" disk for the head joint and a 1" disk for the neck joint. The difference in the disk sizes will help create a wide face. Close the neck edge on the head with spider web stitch (see page 52). Attach limbs and head to body, referring to "Cotter-Pin Joints" on pages 46–47. Stuff and close openings.

FACE: Referring to pages 35–44, install eyes, trim muzzle, embroider nose and mouth, and attach ears.

FINISHING: Brush and steam the mohair fur to smooth out seams. Give your bear a big hug!

# BUNNY SUIT

## MATERIALS

- ¼ yd. white flannel for suit
- 6" square of pink flannel for ear lining and shoe soles
- ½ yd. of ⅛"-wide ribbon
- 2" circle of fur for tail
- ½ yd. of ⅛"-wide elastic
- 1" of ¾"-wide Velcro

## DIRECTIONS FOR BUNNY SUIT

*All seam allowances are ⅛".*

1. Cut two 3½" pieces of elastic for sleeves. Stretch and pin elastic in place and fold raw edge of sleeve piece at wrist over elastic. Sew in place with a straight stitch or zigzag stitch. Sew underarm seam. Repeat for other sleeve.

Sleeve

Pin elastic.

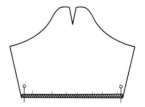

Fold over edge and stitch.

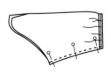

Stitch underarm seam.

2.  Cut two 4" pieces of elastic for legs. Sew elastic to leg in the same manner as for sleeves. Sew leg inseam. Repeat for other leg.

3.  Sew sleeves into opening on body pieces. Sew dart at top of each sleeve. Sew body pieces together from front neck to mark on back. Hem both sides of back opening; then hem neck edge. Cut one piece of Velcro ¼" wide and sew to top of back opening.

Fig. 80. Turn and stitch raw edges.

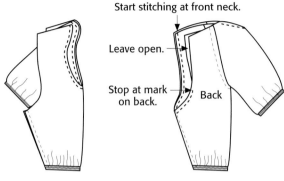

Start stitching at front neck.

Leave open.

Stop at mark on back.

Back

Stitch sleeve to body.     Sew body pieces together.

4.  Gather 2" circle of fur tightly and sew to back of bunny suit. Cut a 12" piece of ribbon. Tie ribbon into a bow with long tails and attach to front neck of suit.

Fig. 81. Stitch bunny ears in back of ear holes.

## Directions for Bunny Suit Hat

1.  Sew hat gusset to hat side head pieces. Hem neck edge and face opening (see fig. 80).

2.  Sew together 1 pink and 1 white ear piece. Turn ear right side out. Repeat for other ear.

3.  Try hat on bear and mark ear locations. Cut a straight line on the hat for each bear ear to fit through. Fold bottom corners of bunny ear to meet in the middle and sew to back side of cut hole (see fig. 81).

4.  Cut one piece of Velcro ¼" wide and sew to chin on hat.

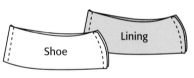

Shoe     Lining

Stitch toe and heel seams.

## Directions for Bunny Suit Shoes

1.  Sew 2 shoe sides together at heel and toe. Repeat with 2 more pieces for lining. With right sides together, put shoe into the lining. Match heels and toes and top raw edges. Sew around top edge. Turn lining to inside of shoe along seam line (see fig. 82). Repeat for other shoe.

2.  Pin shoe sole to raw edges of shoe, matching toes and heels. With sole on top, sew in place (see fig. 83). Repeat for other shoe. The sole is sewn into shoe in same manner as foot pads are sewn into legs. Refer to "Foot Pads" on page 28.

3.  Turn shoes to right side. Tie 2 small bows and sew 1 to front of each shoe.

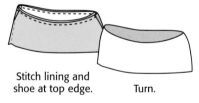

Stitch lining and shoe at top edge.     Turn.

Fig. 82

Fig. 83

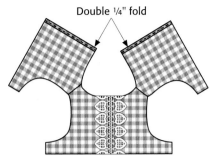

Double ¼" fold

Fig. 84

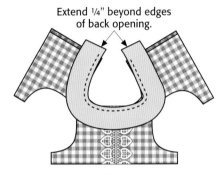

Extend ¼" beyond edges
of back opening.

Fig. 85

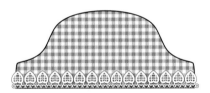

Fig. 86. Match edges and sew
lace to base of sleeve.

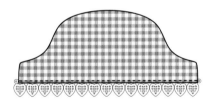

Fig. 87. Turn under hem and stitch in place.

Fig. 88

# RED DRESS AND PANTIES

## MATERIALS

* ⅛ yd. red-check cotton fabric
* 1 yd. of ⅜"-wide, white-cotton heart trim
* 1 yd. of ⅛"-wide elastic
* 3 baby buttons
* 1" of ¾"-wide Velcro

## CUTTING

From red-check fabric, cut the following pieces in addition to the pattern pieces:

* 2½" x 20" strip for skirt
* 1¼" x 6" strip on bias for neck binding

## DIRECTIONS FOR RED DRESS

*All seam allowances are ⅛".*

1. Sew trim to center front of bodice. Sew bodice front and backs together at shoulder seams. Hem each side of back opening (see fig. 84).

2. With right sides together, sew bias neck binding around neck edge. Extend binding ¼" beyond edges of back opening (see fig. 85). Turn binding edge to inside and topstitch.

3. Cut two 7" pieces of heart lace. Sew lace to bottom edge of each sleeve, with raw edges aligned and right side of sleeve fabric facing up (see fig. 86). Fold and turn under hem and raw edge of lace; stitch in place (see fig. 87).

4. Gather top of sleeve to fit armhole, and sew the sleeve in place. Repeat for other sleeve. Cut two 5"-long pieces of ⅛" elastic. Stretching the elastic to fit, sew elastic along line indicated on sleeve pattern. Sew sleeve and body side seams.

5. Cut one 20" piece of heart lace. As with the sleeves, sew lace to bottom edge of skirt, with raw edges aligned. Then fold and turn under hem and raw edge of lace; stitch in place as for sleeve. Sew short edges of skirt strip together, from bottom edge to 1" from top. Fold remaining seam allowances inside. Gather top of skirt strip to fit bodice, and sew in place.

6. Cut three ¼" pieces of Velcro and sew to back opening. Sew 3 baby buttons on top of lace on bodice front.

## DIRECTIONS FOR PANTIES

1. Cut two 4" pieces of ⅛" elastic. Turn bottom edge of a leg to inside to make a ¼"-wide casing, and sew around leg. Insert elastic and pin at each end to secure. Sew leg seam, catching elastic in the stitching (see fig. 88). Repeat for other leg. With right sides together, sew 2 leg pieces together from front to back.

2. Cut one 8" piece of ⅛" elastic. Fold waistband to inside to make ¼"-wide casing, and sew around waist. Leave an opening for elastic. Insert elastic and secure ends. Stitch opening closed (see fig. 89).

Fig. 89

# JEANS

## MATERIALS

* ¼ yd. denim
* 8" piece of ⅛"-wide elastic

## DIRECTIONS

*All seam allowances are ⅛".*

1. Sew front seam from waist to crotch. Do not sew back seam yet.

2. Fold waistband to inside to make a ⅜"-wide casing and sew around. Insert elastic, and pin at each end to secure. Sew back seam from waist to crotch. Backstitch over edges of elastic.

3. Zigzag the raw edges of the pant legs. Sew leg inseam. Roll up cuff.

# BLOUSE

## MATERIALS

* ⅛ yd. light print
* 8" square of contrasting print
* 3 baby buttons
* 1" of ¾"-wide Velcro

From the contrasting print, cut the following pieces in addition to the pattern pieces:

* 2 strips, 1½" x 3¼", for blouse fronts
* 2 strips, 1½" x 7", for sleeves

## DIRECTIONS

*All seam allowances are ⅛".*

1. With wrong sides together, fold all four 1½"-wide strips in half lengthwise. Pin the 3¼"-long strips to wrong side of blouse fronts and sew with a ¼"-wide seam allowance. Fold strips to right side at the seam line. Topstitch in place (see fig. 90).

2. With wrong sides together, fold pocket in half on the fold line and stitch all around. Make a small slit in one layer of pocket. Turn pocket to right side through slit. Pin pocket on left blouse front and topstitch in place.

3. Sew fronts and back together at shoulder seams.

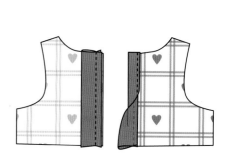

Fig. 90

Fig. 91

4. Repeat step 1 with 7"-long strips on straight, raw edges of sleeves.

5. With right sides facing, sew 2 collar pieces together, leaving neck edge open. Turn to right side. Repeat for other collar. Starting ¼" from front opening, pin each collar in place around neck; they should meet at middle of back neck. Sew collars in place (see fig. 91).

6. Gather top edge of sleeve to fit armhole. Sew in place. Repeat for other sleeve. Sew underarm and side seams.

7. Hem bottom edge of blouse.

8. Cut three ¼"-wide pieces of Velcro. Sew in place on front of blouse. Sew buttons on front placket.

# BLACK SHOES AND RED SHOES WITH STRAP

## MATERIALS

For each pair of shoes:

* 6" square of upholstery velvet
* 4" square of matching felt
* 2 snaps (for red shoes only)
* 2 small buttons (for red shoes only)

## DIRECTIONS

*All seam allowances are ⅛".*

1. Sew 2 shoe sides together at toe and heel seam. Be sure to backstitch at beginning and ending of seam. Sew shoe sole to shoe in same manner as foot pads. Refer to "Foot Pads" on page 28. Repeat for other shoe.

2. For strap on red shoes: Cut 2 strips, each ¼" x 3", from upholstery velvet. Fold one end under ¼" and sew to inside edge at the middle of shoe side. Place strap at a slight angle so that it will wrap around the front of the bear ankle.

3. On opposite end of strap, cut both corners at an angle to make a point. Sew snap to wrong side of pointed end of strap and to middle of other side of shoe. Sew button to right side of shoe strap above snap (see fig. 92). Repeat for other shoe, making sure to make one left and one right shoe.

Fig. 92

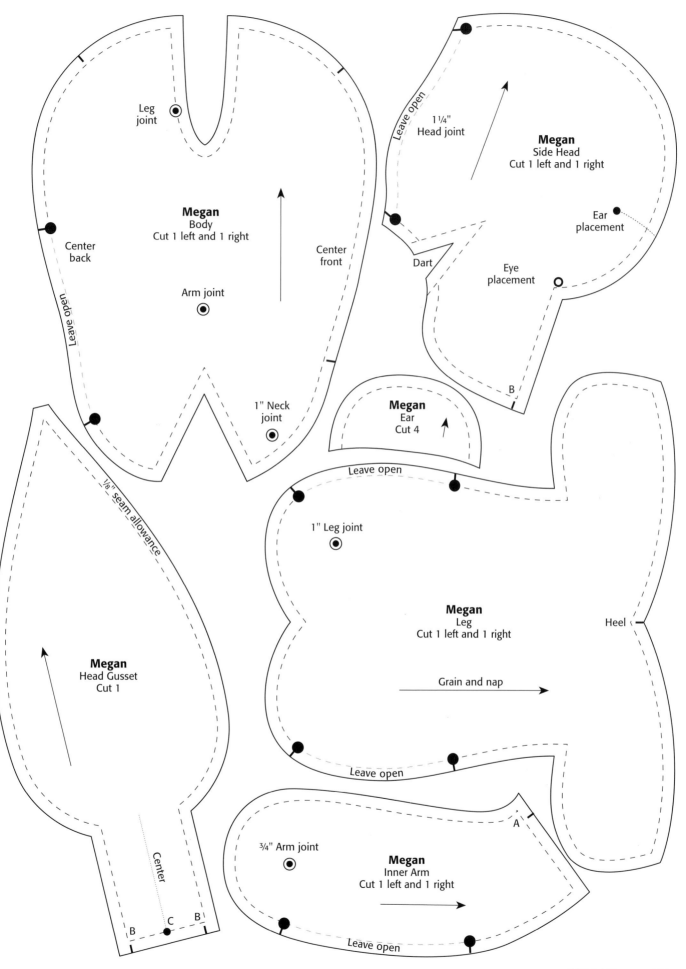

Leg joint

**Megan**
Body
Cut 1 left and 1 right

Center back

Leave open

Arm joint

Center front

1" Neck joint

Leave open

Leave open
1¼" Head joint

**Megan**
Side Head
Cut 1 left and 1 right

Ear placement

Dart

Eye placement

B

**Megan**
Ear
Cut 4

⅛" seam allowance

Leave open

1" Leg joint

**Megan**
Leg
Cut 1 left and 1 right

Heel

**Megan**
Head Gusset
Cut 1

Grain and nap

Leave open

Center

B    C    B

¾" Arm joint

**Megan**
Inner Arm
Cut 1 left and 1 right

A

Leave open

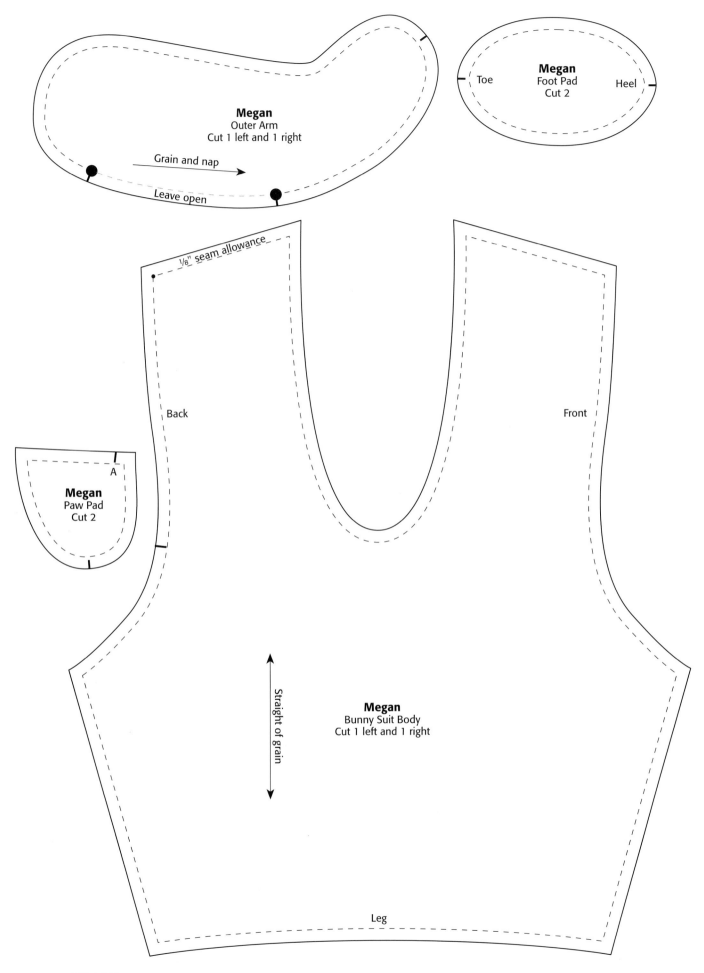

**Megan**
Outer Arm
Cut 1 left and 1 right

Grain and nap →

Leave open

**Megan**
Foot Pad
Cut 2

Toe          Heel

⅛" seam allowance

Back

Front

A

**Megan**
Paw Pad
Cut 2

Straight of grain

**Megan**
Bunny Suit Body
Cut 1 left and 1 right

Leg

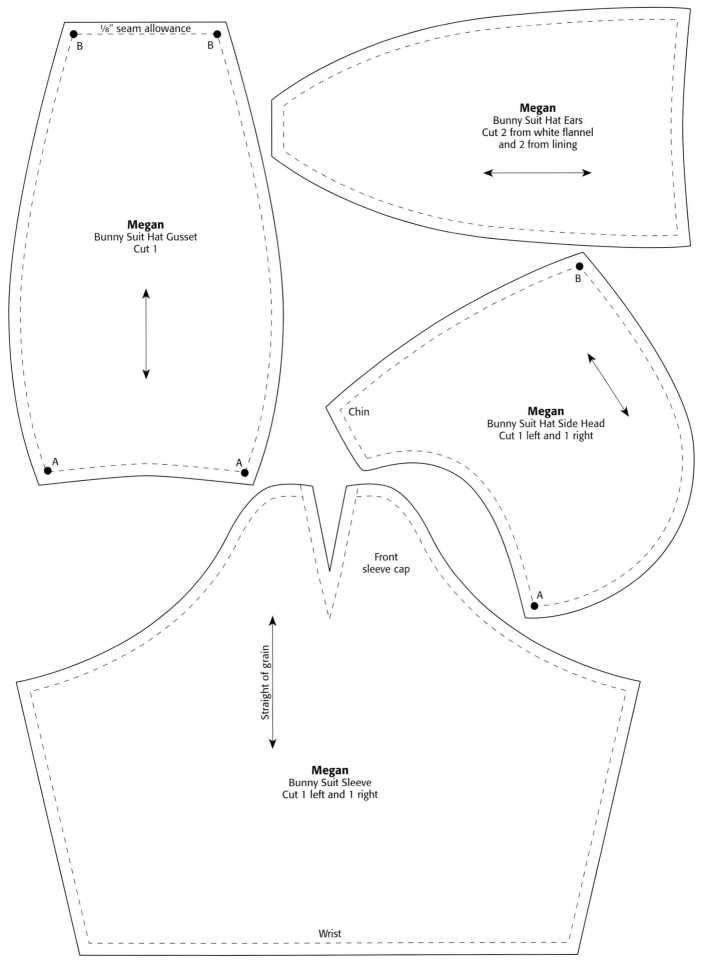

⅛" seam allowance

B          B

**Megan**
Bunny Suit Hat Gusset
Cut 1

A          A

**Megan**
Bunny Suit Hat Ears
Cut 2 from white flannel
and 2 from lining

B

Chin

**Megan**
Bunny Suit Hat Side Head
Cut 1 left and 1 right

A

Front
sleeve cap

Straight of grain

**Megan**
Bunny Suit Sleeve
Cut 1 left and 1 right

Wrist

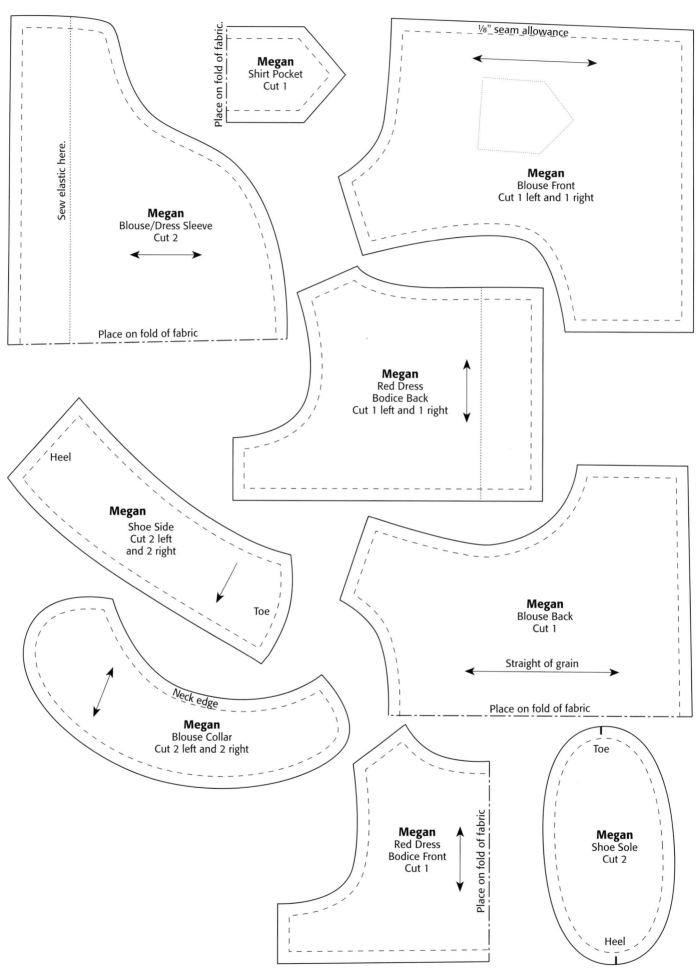

Place on fold of fabric.

**Megan**
Shirt Pocket
Cut 1

⅛" seam allowance

**Megan**
Blouse Front
Cut 1 left and 1 right

Sew elastic here.

**Megan**
Blouse/Dress Sleeve
Cut 2

Place on fold of fabric

**Megan**
Red Dress
Bodice Back
Cut 1 left and 1 right

Heel

**Megan**
Shoe Side
Cut 2 left
and 2 right

Toe

**Megan**
Blouse Back
Cut 1

Straight of grain

Place on fold of fabric

Neck edge

**Megan**
Blouse Collar
Cut 2 left and 2 right

**Megan**
Red Dress
Bodice Front
Cut 1

Place on fold of fabric

Toe

**Megan**
Shoe Sole
Cut 2

Heel

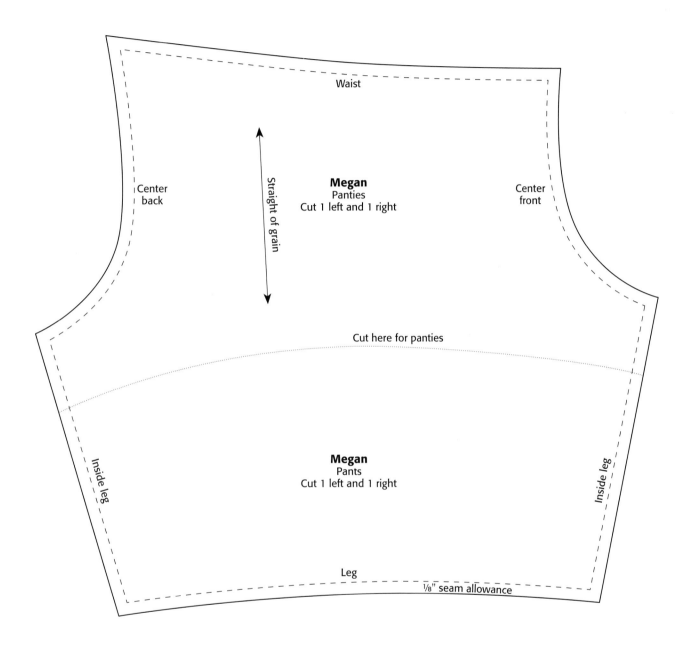

Waist

Center
back

Straight of grain

**Megan**
Panties
Cut 1 left and 1 right

Center
front

Cut here for panties

Inside leg

**Megan**
Pants
Cut 1 left and 1 right

Inside leg

Leg

⅛" seam allowance

# REGGIE

 *Learn to sew foot pads the same way that some old-time manufacturers did them.*

BEAR FACTS: IN 1909, SAMUEL FINSBERG & COMPANY, A BRITISH TOY MANUFACTURER, PRODUCED A FLANNEL, CUTOUT PRINT TO MAKE A TEDDY BEAR. BRITISH CONTRIBUTIONS TO THE TEDDY BEAR WORLD HAVE BEEN STRONG, WITH SEVERAL TOY MANUFACTURERS AND LITERARY BRUINS SUCH AS WINNIE THE POOH, PADDINGTON, AND RUPERT.

*18" Jointed Bear by Linda Mead, 1999, Spare Bear Parts, Interlochen, Michigan*

# MATERIALS

* ⅓ yd. of ¾" straight-pile mohair fur fabric
* 7" x 8" piece of felt for paw pads and foot pads
* 1 pair of 12 mm black glass eyes
* Size 3 perle cotton for nose and mouth
* Beeswax for nose (optional)
* Excelsior or firm-pack polyester stuffing
* Locknut and bolt joints
  * Six 2¼" joint disks for neck and legs
  * Four 1¾" joint disks for arms
  * 5 bolts
  * 5 locknuts

# DIRECTIONS

*All seam allowances are ¼".*

Refer to "Getting Started" on pages 21–24 for making patterns, cutting fabric, and transferring markings.

**GROOMING SEAMS:** After sewing each seam, pull fur out of seams on both wrong and right sides.

**ARMS:** Pin and sew paw pad to inner arm at wrist edge, matching marks. Fold arm right sides together, match marks, and pin. Sew around arm, leaving an opening as marked. Repeat for other arm.

**LEGS:** Pin 2 leg pieces together, matching all marks. Starting at toe, sew around the leg to upper "Leave open" mark. Then match and pin toe mark on foot pad to toe seam of leg. Match heel mark on foot pad to heel mark on one side of leg and pin. Starting at heel, sew to toe. Pivot at toe and realign foot pad and leg. Sew from toe to heel and continue up back of leg to bottom "Leave open" mark. Repeat for other leg.

**BODY:** Pin 1 front and 1 back piece together at side seam, matching all marks. Sew from neck edge to bottom point. Repeat for remaining front and back pieces. Pin body halves together, matching all marks. Sew from back neck to the upper "Leave open" mark. Sew from the front neck, down front, and around bottom to lower "Leave open" mark. Use a long running stitch to gather neck edge.

**HEAD WITH ROUNDED MUZZLE** (page 30): Pin side head pieces together, matching A marks. Sew from nose (A), down chin seam to neck edge. Pin gusset to a side head piece, matching A marks. With gusset on top, sew from nose to back neck. Repeat with other side head piece. Use contrasting thread for tailor tacks to mark ear and eye placements on outside of head.

## ARTIST TIP

Create your own nose pattern shape from self-adhesive craft felt, or buy a precut nose shape sold under the trade name "Nose Templates." The adhesive will hold the felt in place while you embroider the nose over it. The felt adds thickness and makes a good pattern to keep your stitches even. Embroidering a perfect nose takes practice. Until you are able to stitch a perfect nose, you can hide any unevenness along the top or bottom edge of the stitches by passing the needle through the perle cotton across the line of stitches. You will actually split the perle cotton thread.

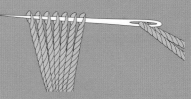

## ABOUT THE PATTERN

Reggie was designed with long straight legs and a thin body to wear clothes. The pattern also has an unusual method to sew the foot pad. If you prefer an old-looking bear, leave the fur in the stitch line of the head gusset.

**EARS:** Pin and sew 2 ear pieces together along curved edges, leaving straight edges open. Repeat for other ear.

**JOINTING AND STUFFING:** For a reproduction of a vintage bear, stuff with excelsior. Refer to "Locknut and Bolt (or Tap-Bolt) Joints" on pages 47–48 for the head. After stuffing head and inserting assembled joint, close neck opening on head with spider web stitch (page 52). Attach limbs with locknut and bolt joints. Stuff limbs and body, and close openings.

**FACE:** Referring to pages 35–44, install eyes, trim muzzle, embroider nose and mouth, and attach ears. If desired, use a piece of sand paper on the black glass eyes to dull the finish and duplicate the look of old leather shoe buttons.

**FINISHING:** Brush the fur with a wire brush, especially at the seams. Give your bear a big hug!

# TURTLENECK

## MATERIAL
* ¼ yd. rib knit

## CUTTING
From knit fabric, cut the following piece in addition to the pattern pieces:
* 1 strip, 6" x 11", for collar

NOTE: *When sewing stretchy fabrics, stretch the seams slightly as you sew.*

## DIRECTIONS
*All seam allowances are ¼".*

1. Sew front and back together at shoulder seams.

2. Sew 6" ends of collar strip together to form a circle.

3. On body, divide neck edge into quarters and mark with pins. Repeat for collar.

4. With right sides together, pin a single layer of collar to neck edge, matching pins. Sew collar to neck, stretching as necessary to match neck edge.

5. Sew sleeves into arm openings. Sew sleeve seam and side seam. Do not hem bottom edges of sleeves or body.

6. Fold collar in thirds so that edge of collar covers neck seam. Fold sleeves to make cuffs.

# PANTS

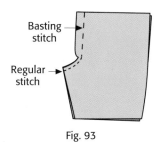

Fig. 93

## MATERIALS

* ¼ yd. plaid
* One ½"-diameter button
* 3 snaps

## CUTTING

From plaid, cut the following pieces in addition to the pattern pieces:

* 2" x 17" strip for waistband
* 1" x 18" strip for belt loops

Fig. 94. Topstitch.

## DIRECTIONS

*All seam allowances are ¼".*

1. With wrong sides together, fold pocket in half on the fold line and stitch all around. Make a small slit in one layer of pocket. Turn pocket right sides out through slit. Sew button at top edge. Pin pocket on one side of back pants, with right side up. Topstitch in place.

2. Baste 2 front pieces together from waist to crotch along the dashed line for the fly, and sew a regular stitch along the crotch (as indicated on pattern). See figure 93.

3. Press fly open. Topstitch half of fly into position. Remove basting stitches. Tack pleats at waist (see fig. 94).

4. Sew 2 back pieces together from waist to crotch. Sew front and back together at side seams.

5. Hem each leg. Sew inseam of pants.

6. Fold 1" x 18" strip lengthwise in thirds and topstitch down the center. Cut strip into 9 pieces, each 2" long. Pin one end of belt loops to right side of waist, distributing them evenly along waist edge.

7. With right sides together, pin one edge of waistband to waist, extending waistband ½" beyond edge of front openings (see fig. 95). Sew waistband to waist. Fold ends right sides together and sew closed (see fig. 96).

8. Turn ends right side out, pin waistband in position, and pin loose ends of belt loops to inside of waist. Stitch in the ditch from the top, catching the edge of the waistband underneath and the ends of the belt loops (see fig. 97).

9. Sew snaps at waist and along fly.

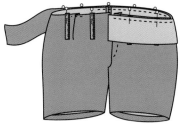

Fig. 95

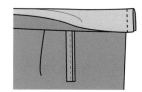

Fig. 96. Fold ends together and stitch closed.

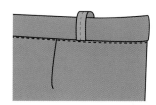

Fig. 97

# Belt

## Materials

* ⅜" x 18" strip of black velvet upholstery fabric or other non-ravel fabric
* Doll belt buckle or watch buckle to fit ⅜"-wide belt

1. Attach buckle to fabric strip.

2. Poke hole in opposite end of fabric strip for buckle post (see fig. 98).

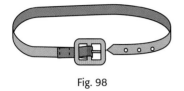

Fig. 98

# Shoes

## Materials

* ⅛ yd. upholstery velvet or other non-ravel fabric for shoe sides and tongues
* 6" square of felt for soles
* 1 shoelace
* Metal eyelets for shoelace holes (optional)

## Directions

*All seam allowances are ¼".*

1. Sew dart in tongue. Repeat for other tongue.

2. Pin wrong side of facing to wrong side of shoe side. Topstitch around facing. Repeat for other shoe side. Sew heel seam. Finger-press heel seam allowance open and topstitch along each side of seam (see fig. 99).

3. Pin shoe sides to sole, matching heel seam to heel mark. Pin tongue with dart centered on toe mark (see fig. 100).

   With sole on top, sew all around sole with ¼"-wide seam allowance. Trim seam allowance to ⅛".

4. Install 3 metal eyelets on each side following package directions, or cut holes with small paper punch (see fig. 101). Cut shoelace in half and tie shoe. Repeat to make other shoe.

Fig. 99

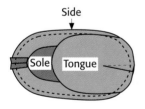

Fig. 100

Fig. 101

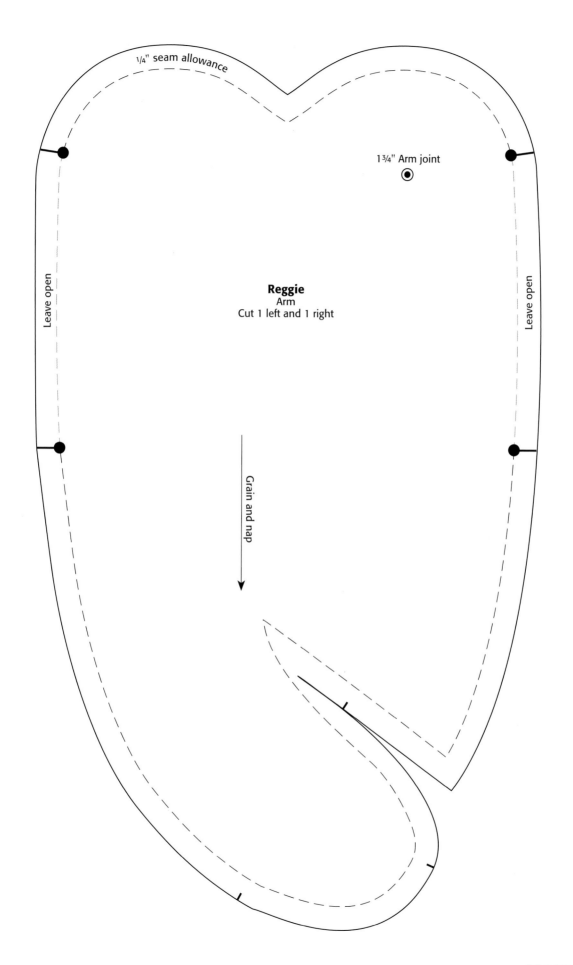

¼" seam allowance

1¾" Arm joint
⊙

Leave open

**Reggie**
Arm
Cut 1 left and 1 right

Leave open

Grain and nap

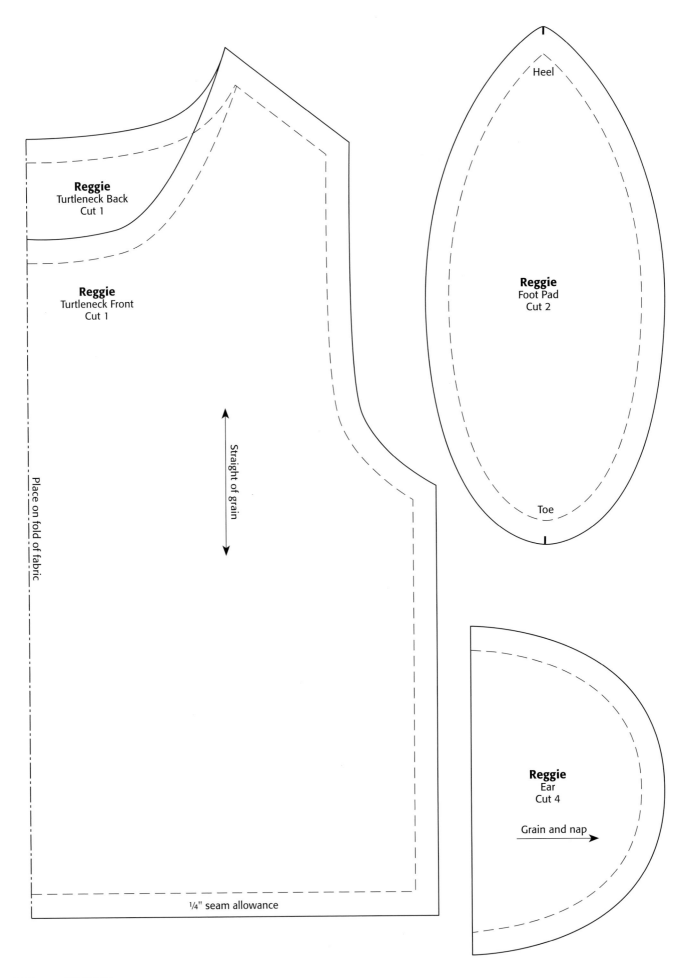

**Reggie**
Turtleneck Back
Cut 1

**Reggie**
Turtleneck Front
Cut 1

Straight of grain

Place on fold of fabric

¼" seam allowance

Heel

**Reggie**
Foot Pad
Cut 2

Toe

**Reggie**
Ear
Cut 4

Grain and nap

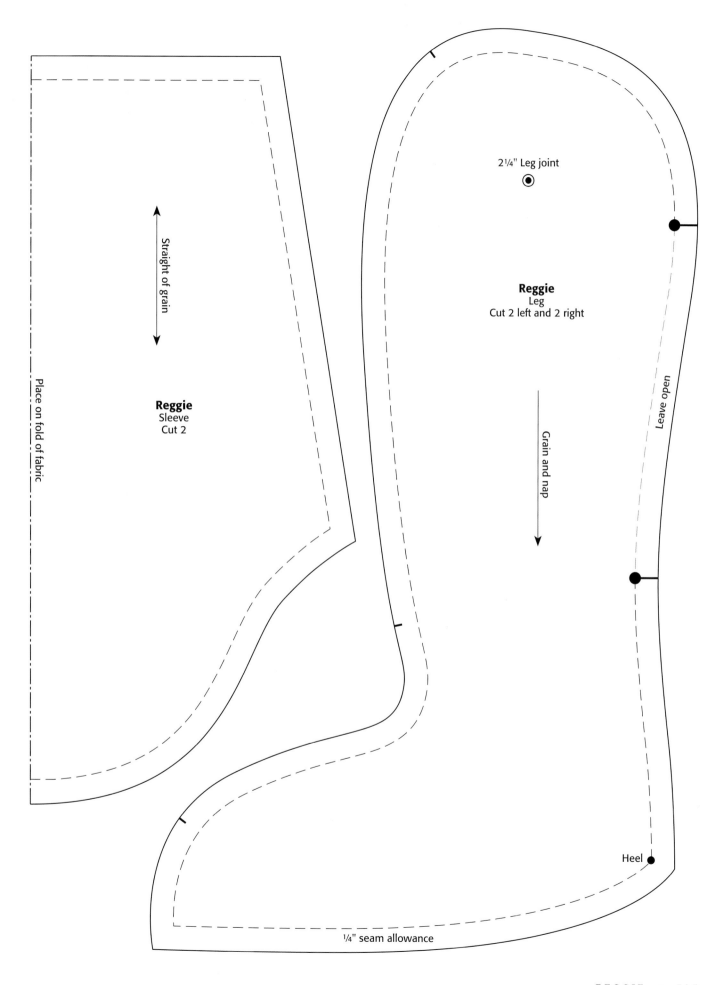

Straight of grain

Place on fold of fabric

**Reggie**
Sleeve
Cut 2

2¼" Leg joint

**Reggie**
Leg
Cut 2 left and 2 right

Grain and nap

Leave open

Heel

¼" seam allowance

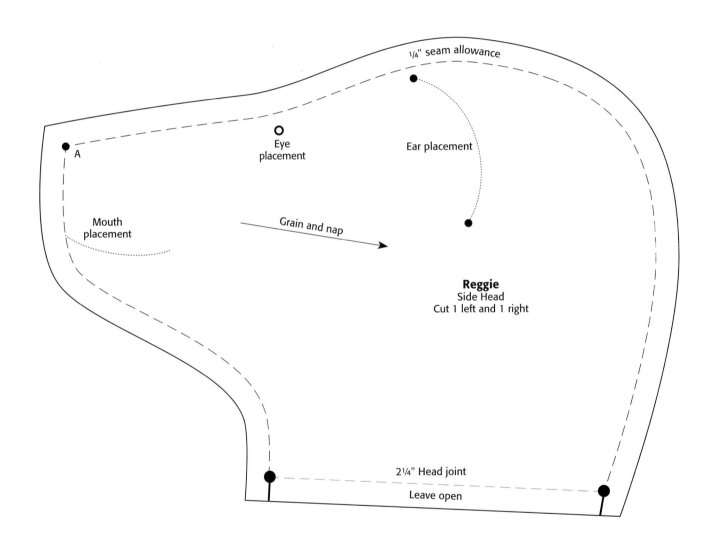

¹/₄" seam allowance

Eye
placement

Ear placement

A

Mouth
placement

Grain and nap

**Reggie**
Side Head
Cut 1 left and 1 right

2¹/₄" Head joint

Leave open

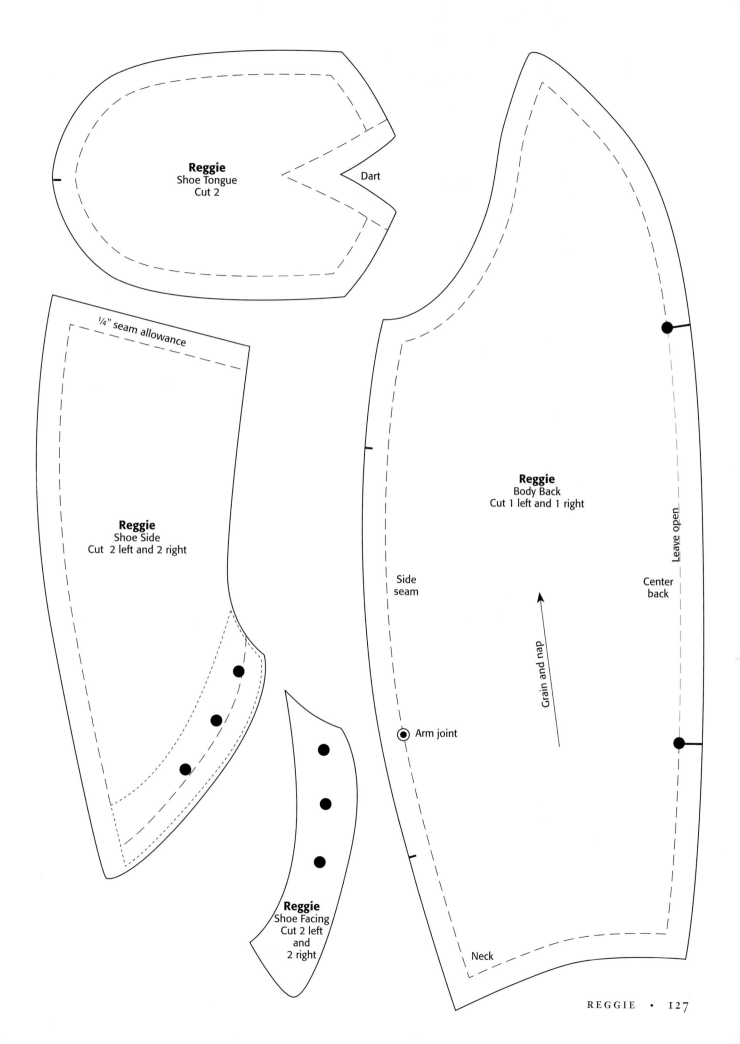

**Reggie**
Shoe Tongue
Cut 2

Dart

¼" seam allowance

**Reggie**
Shoe Side
Cut 2 left and 2 right

**Reggie**
Shoe Facing
Cut 2 left
and
2 right

**Reggie**
Body Back
Cut 1 left and 1 right

Side
seam

Leave open

Center
back

Grain and nap

Arm joint

Neck

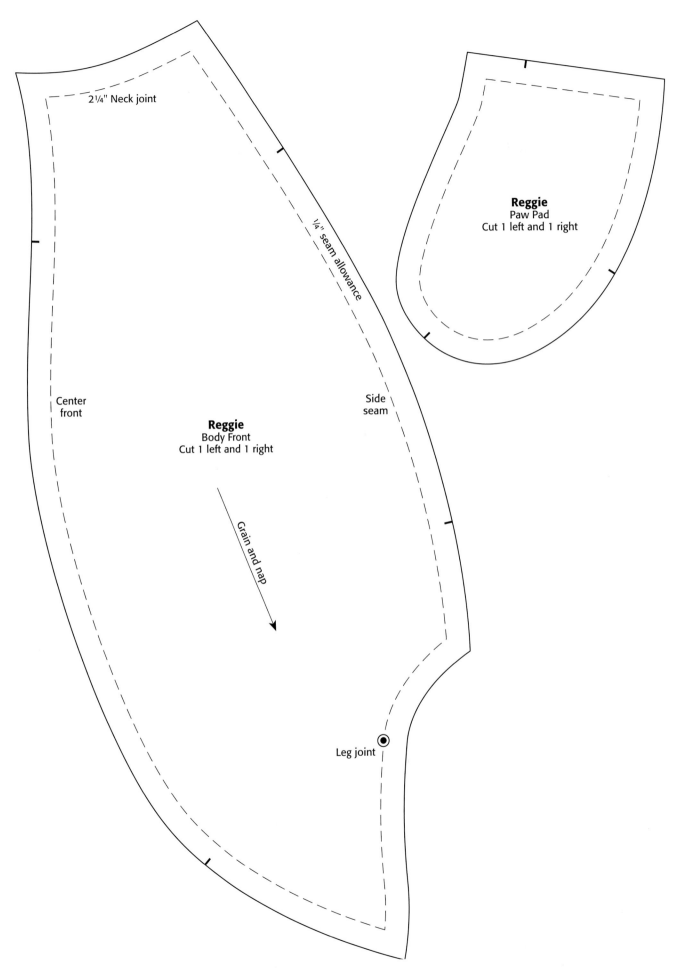

2¼" Neck joint

¼" seam allowance

**Reggie**
Paw Pad
Cut 1 left and 1 right

Center
front

Side
seam

**Reggie**
Body Front
Cut 1 left and 1 right

Grain and nap

Leg joint

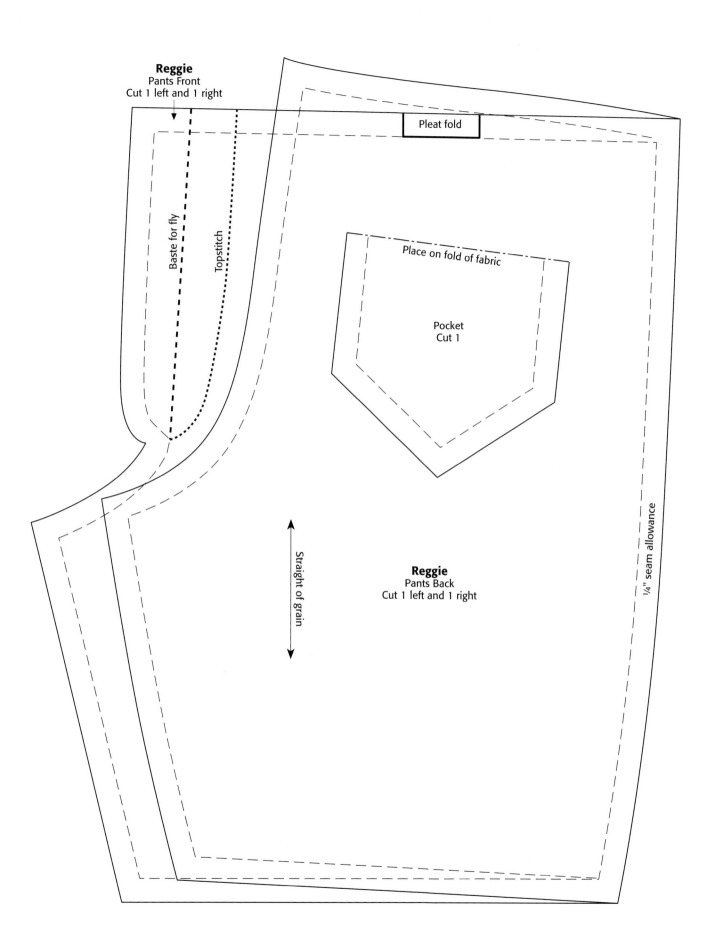

**Reggie**
Pants Front
Cut 1 left and 1 right

Baste for fly

Topstitch

Pleat fold

Place on fold of fabric

Pocket
Cut 1

Straight of grain

**Reggie**
Pants Back
Cut 1 left and 1 right

¼" seam allowance

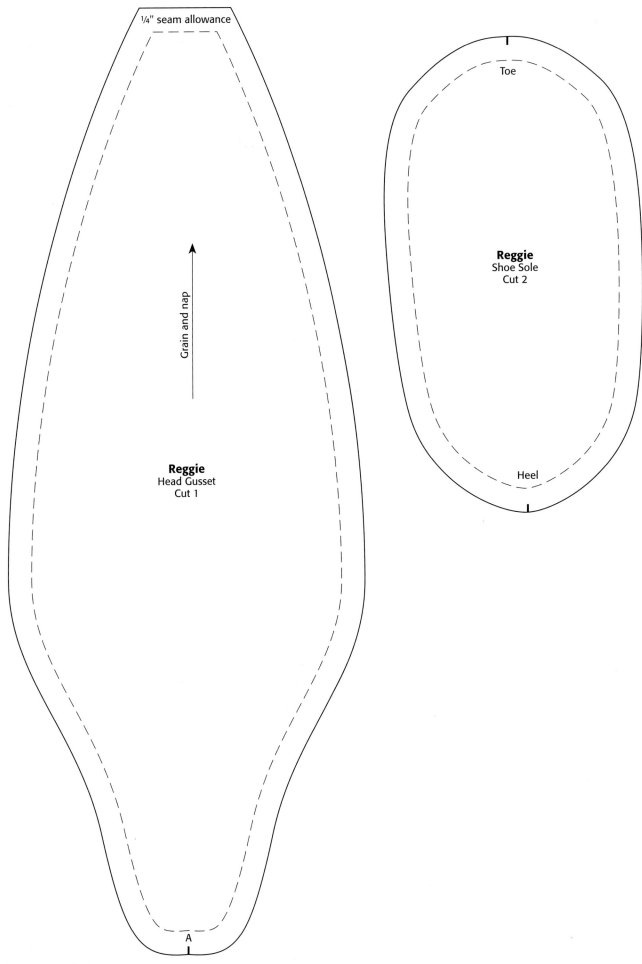

¼" seam allowance

Grain and nap

**Reggie**
Head Gusset
Cut 1

A

**Reggie**
Shoe Sole
Cut 2

Toe

Heel

# MY CHILDHOOD FRIEND

🐾 🐾    *Make this easy thread-jointed bear.*

🐾 🐾 🐾    *Learn how to use special treatments to age a bear.*

BEAR FACTS: ACCORDING TO *THE GUINNESS BOOK OF WORLD RECORDS*, THE MOST EXPENSIVE BEAR SOLD AT AUCTION WAS A 1926 DUAL (TWO-TONED/TIPPED) MOHAIR PLUSH STEIFF. THE WINNING BID OF $86,350 WAS MADE BY PAUL VOLPP, WHO BOUGHT THE BEAR IN 1986 AS AN ANNIVERSARY GIFT TO HIS WIFE, ROSEMARY. SHE NAMED IT HAPPY.

*10" Thread-Jointed Bear by Linda Mead, 1999, Spare Bear Parts, Interlochen, Michigan*

## ABOUT THE PATTERN

This small bear, with its low forehead, long and narrow feet, and arms that are longer than the legs, is reminiscent of the earliest teddy bears. By using excelsior for stuffing and jointing with string, you could almost mistake it for an genuine antique!

# MATERIALS

* ¼ yd. of ¼"-pile, ultra-sparse mohair
* 5" x 4" piece of felt for paw pads and foot pads
* 1 pair of 5 mm black glass eyes
* Size 3 perle cotton for nose and mouth
* Excelsior
* Optional
  * Beeswax for nose
  * Sandpaper to distress eyes
  * 1 box each of Rit Dye in taupe and dark green
  * Rubber gloves
  * 2 quart jar

# DIRECTIONS

*All seam allowances are ¼", except for ⅛" seam allowances on foot pads.*

Refer to "Getting Started" on pages 21–24 for making patterns, cutting fabric, and transferring markings.

**GROOMING SEAMS:** If you prefer an old-looking bear, do not pull the fur out of the seams after sewing.

**ARMS:** Pin and sew paw pad to inner arm at wrist edge, matching marks. Fold arm right sides together, match all marks, and pin. Sew around arm, leaving an opening as marked. Repeat for other arm.

**LEGS:** Fold leg with right sides together, match marks, and pin. Starting at toe, sew around the leg. Leave an opening at the top as marked and at the bottom for the foot pad. Match and pin toe mark on foot pad to toe seam of leg. Match and pin heel mark on foot pad to heel mark on leg. Pin foot pad to each side of leg. Place additional pins between these 4 pins as needed to keep the raw edges of the foot pad and leg even and the fullness equally distributed. With the foot pad face up, sew around foot with a ⅛"-wide seam allowance. Refer to "Foot Pads" on page 28. Repeat for other leg.

**BODY:** Pin 1 front and 1 back piece together at side seam, matching all marks. Sew from neck edge to bottom corner. Repeat for remaining front and back pieces. Pin body halves together, matching all marks. Starting at "Leave open" mark on upper back, sew around hump, down front, and around bottom to "Leave open" mark on lower back.

**HEAD WITH ROUNDED MUZZLE** (page 30): Pin and sew the side head pieces together from nose, down chin to neck edge. Pin head gusset to a side head piece, matching mark on gusset to chin seam. With gusset on top, sew from nose to end of gusset. Repeat with other side head piece.

Finish seam from end of gusset to neck edge, if necessary. Leave the neck edge open. Use contrasting thread for tailor tacks to mark ear and eye placements on outside of head.

**EARS:** Pin and sew 2 ear pieces together along curved edges, leaving straight edges open. Repeat for other ear.

**STUFFING:** Stuff head, packing muzzle area very firmly. As you stuff, mold face with your hands. Close neck edge on head with spider web stitch (page 52). Stuff limbs and body, and sew openings closed.

**JOINTING:** Attach head and limbs to body, referring to "Thread Jointing" on pages 52–53.

**FACE:** Referring to pages 35–44, install eyes, trim muzzle, embroider nose and mouth, and attach ears. Tie off threads for eyes under ears.

**AGING YOUR BEAR:** Pluck patches of fur to thin it out and to make bald spots. Use sandpaper to dull the finish of the glass eyes. Cut holes in felt pads and fur fabric so excelsior shows. Referring to "Artist Tip" on page 132, dab dye onto excelsior and in patches around fabric, leaving some areas undyed. Wrap bear in several layers of paper towels and squeeze out excess dye. Set bear aside to dry or use hair dryer. Do not brush fur. Sew small flannel patches on bear as desired.

**FINISHING:** Add a ribbon around the neck, if desired. Give your new bear a big hug!

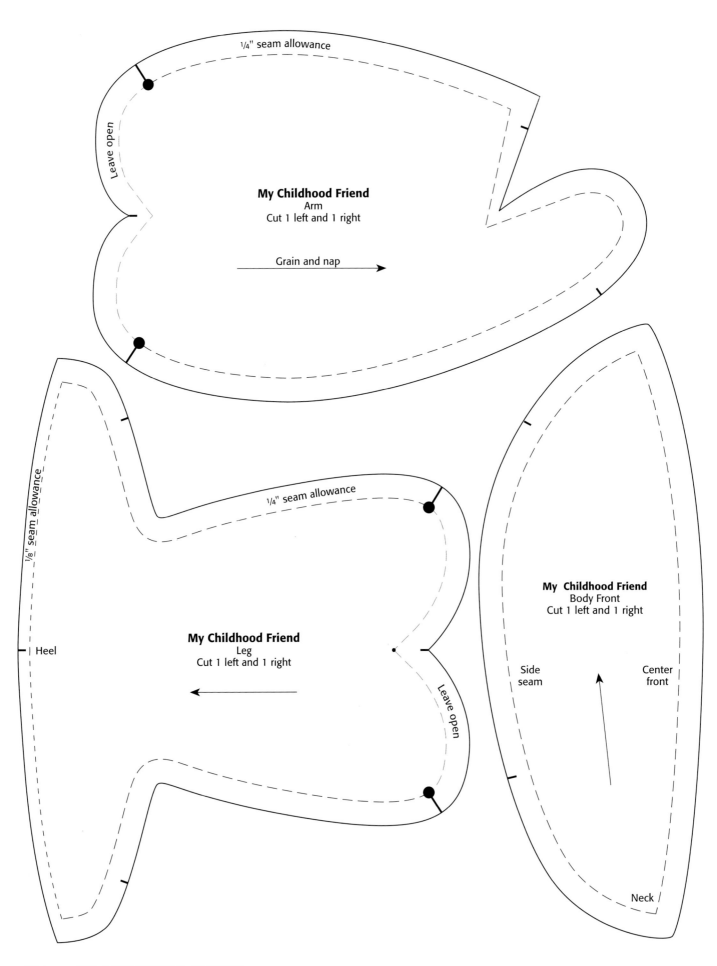

1/4" seam allowance

Leave open

**My Childhood Friend**
Arm
Cut 1 left and 1 right

Grain and nap

1/8" seam allowance

1/4" seam allowance

Heel

**My Childhood Friend**
Leg
Cut 1 left and 1 right

Leave open

**My Childhood Friend**
Body Front
Cut 1 left and 1 right

Side
seam

Center
front

Neck

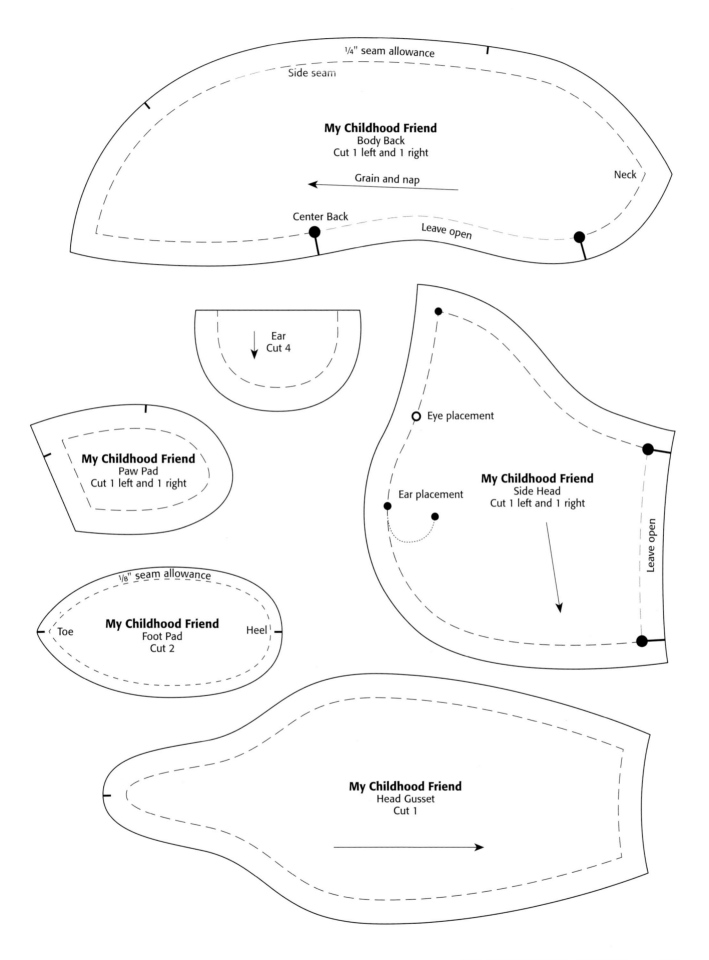

¼" seam allowance

Side seam

**My Childhood Friend**
Body Back
Cut 1 left and 1 right

Grain and nap

Center Back

Leave open

Neck

Ear
Cut 4

**My Childhood Friend**
Paw Pad
Cut 1 left and 1 right

Eye placement

Ear placement

**My Childhood Friend**
Side Head
Cut 1 left and 1 right

Leave open

⅛" seam allowance

Toe

Heel

**My Childhood Friend**
Foot Pad
Cut 2

**My Childhood Friend**
Head Gusset
Cut 1

# CORKY

  *Make an easy traditional bear.*

 *See "Artist Tip" for help in designing your own patterns.*

BEAR FACTS: TEDDY BEAR MANUFACTURING HAS ALWAYS BEEN A COTTAGE INDUSTRY, STARTING WITH MARGARET STEIFF WORKING FROM HER HOME, TO TODAY'S MANY ARTISTS WHO PARTICIPATE IN THE THOUSANDS OF TEDDY BEAR SHOWS WORLDWIDE. THE MOST OUTSTANDING DESIGNS HAVE BEEN FROM INDIVIDUALS. THE FUTURE OF TEDDY BEAR DESIGNING IS LIMITED ONLY BY ARTIST IMAGINATION.

*15" Jointed Bear by Linda Mead, 1999, Spare Bear Parts, Interlochen, Michigan*

# MATERIALS

* ⅓ yd. of ¾"-pile mohair fur fabric
* 6" x 7" piece of felt for paw pads
* 1 pair of 12 mm black glass eyes
* Size 3 perle cotton for nose and mouth
* Excelsior to stuff muzzle
* Firm-pack polyester stuffing
* Rivet joints
  * Four 2" joint disks for legs
  * Six 1½" joint disks for head, neck, and arms
  * 10 rivet washers
  * 5 rivets

# DIRECTIONS

*All seam allowances are ¼".*

Refer to "Getting Started" on pages 21–24 for making patterns, cutting fabric, and transferring markings. To make a full leg pattern, place the pattern piece on the fold of a piece of paper, trace, and cut out.

**GROOMING SEAMS:** If you prefer an old-looking bear, leave the fur in the seam line of the head gusset.

**ARMS:** Pin and sew paw pad to inner arm at wrist edge, matching marks. Fold arm right sides together, match marks, and pin. Sew around arm, leaving an opening as marked. Repeat for other arm.

**LEGS:** Fold leg right sides together, match marks, and pin. Starting at toe, sew around the leg. Leave an opening at the top as marked and at bottom for foot pad. Match and pin toe mark on foot pad to toe seam of leg. Match and pin heel mark on foot pad to heel mark on leg. Pin foot pad to each side of leg. Place additional pins between these 4 pins as needed to keep raw edges of foot pad and leg even and the fullness equally distributed. With foot pad on top, sew around foot. Refer to "Foot Pads" on page 28. Repeat for other leg.

**BODY:** Pin 1 front and 1 back piece together at side seam, matching all marks. Sew from neck edge to bottom corner. Repeat for remaining front and back pieces. Pin body halves together, matching all marks. Starting at "Leave open" mark on upper back, sew around hump. Skip a stitch at neck joint mark for joint hardware; then continue down front and around bottom to "Leave open" mark on lower back.

**HEAD WITH ROUNDED MUZZLE** (page 30): Pin and sew the darts on the neck edge of the side head pieces. Pin side head pieces together, matching A mark and chin seam. Sew from nose, down chin, and across to

## ARTIST TIP

Start designing your own teddy bears. Mix several bear patterns to combine the parts you like best. A flexible ruler is a wonderful tool to help you draw curves to make changes to the shape of the pattern. When altering patterns, there is one unbreakable rule: any two pieces sewn together must be altered to match.

## ABOUT THE PATTERN

The bear in the photo was made from the original pattern (solid lines on pattern). The dotted lines indicate places where you can make alterations. When making alterations, it is important to remember that what you do to one piece you must do to adjoining pieces by adding or reducing an equal amount.

You can increase or decrease the tummy, back hump, or any other curved area. Use a flexible ruler to create the desired shape.

You can lengthen or shorten the pieces at the horizontal dotted lines. To shorten the pattern, cut along the dotted line and overlap the two pieces. To lengthen the pattern, spread the two pieces apart at the dotted line and fill in the gap with an extra piece of paper. Draw new lines to complete the pattern.

You can widen or narrow any of the pattern pieces by cutting through the center vertically. Follow the grain line to make the cut, and spread or overlap the pattern pieces.

back neck, skipping a stitch just behind the dart. Pin head gusset to a side head piece, matching A marks. With the gusset on top, sew from the nose (A) to the back of the gusset. Repeat with other side head piece, leaving an opening as marked. Finish seam from end of gusset to neck edge, if necessary. Use contrasting thread for tailor tacks to mark ear and eye placements on outside of head.

**EARS:** Pin and sew 2 ear pieces together along curved edges, leaving straight edges open. Repeat for other ear.

**JOINTING AND STUFFING:** Referring to "Rivet Joints" on pages 49–50, attach limbs and head to body. Stuff after joints are assembled and close openings.

**FACE:** Referring to pages 35–44, install eyes, trim muzzle, embroider nose and mouth, and attach ears.

**FINISHING:** Brush fur with a wire brush, especially at the seams. Tie a ribbon around neck, if desired. Give your new bear a hug!

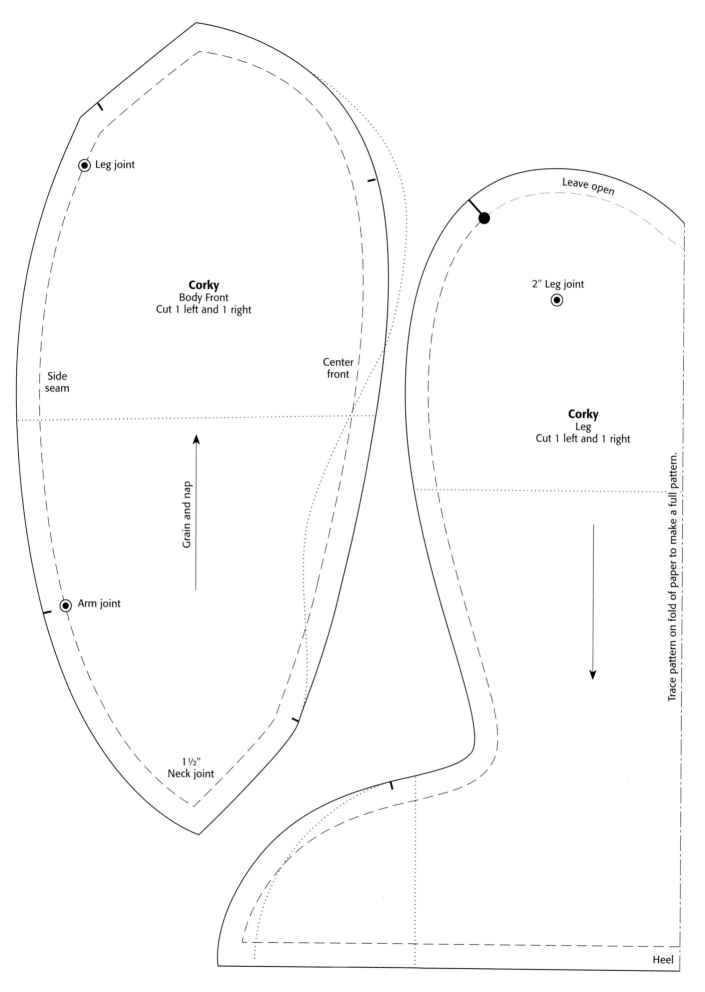

Leg joint

**Corky**
Body Front
Cut 1 left and 1 right

Side
seam

Center
front

Grain and nap

Arm joint

1½"
Neck joint

Leave open

2" Leg joint

**Corky**
Leg
Cut 1 left and 1 right

Trace pattern on fold of paper to make a full pattern.

Heel

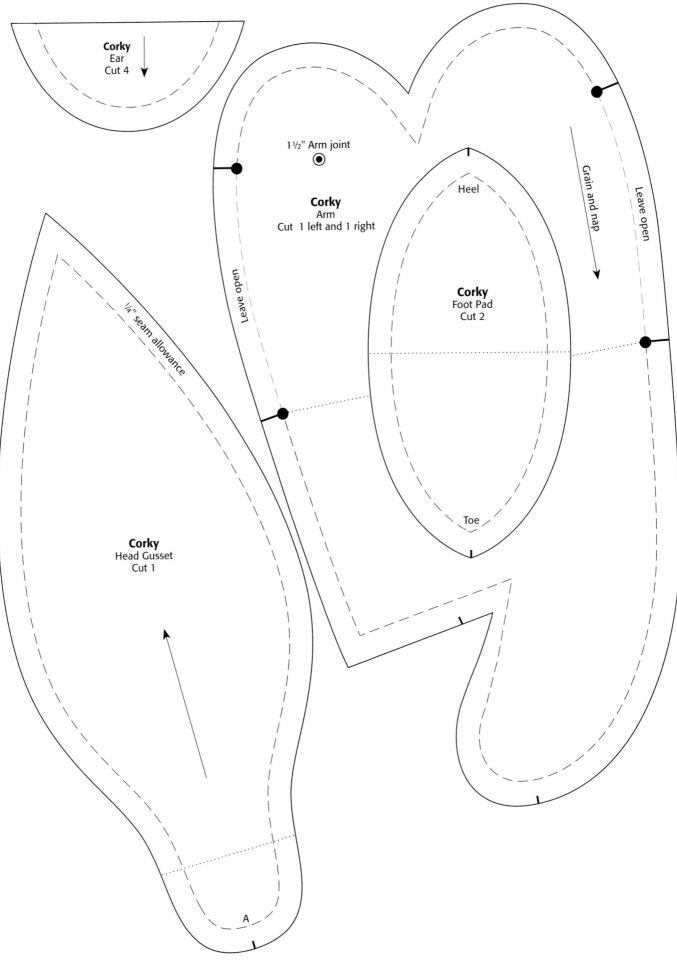

**Corky**
Ear
Cut 4

1½" Arm joint

**Corky**
Arm
Cut 1 left and 1 right

Leave open

Grain and nap

Leave open

Heel

**Corky**
Foot Pad
Cut 2

Toe

¼" seam allowance

**Corky**
Head Gusset
Cut 1

A

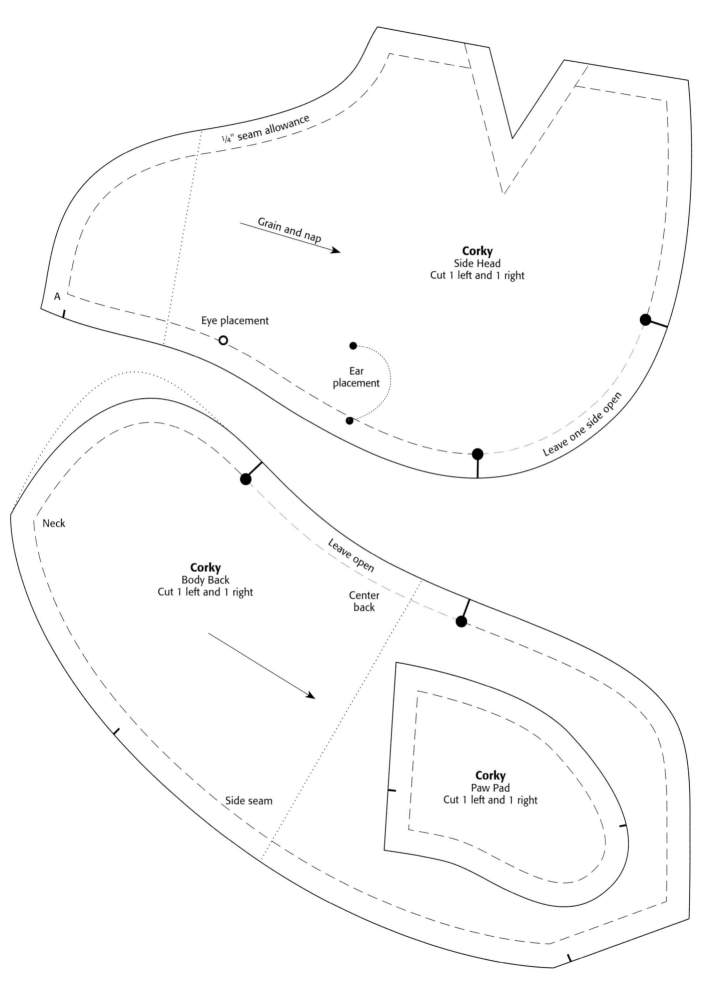

¼" seam allowance

Grain and nap

**Corky**
Side Head
Cut 1 left and 1 right

A

Eye placement

Ear
placement

Leave one side open

Neck

Leave open

**Corky**
Body Back
Cut 1 left and 1 right

Center
back

**Corky**
Paw Pad
Cut 1 left and 1 right

Side seam

# CIRCUS BEAR

  *Advanced bear makers will experience sewing a curved dart and see how it adds fullness to the cheeks when stuffed.*

**BEAR FACTS:**

- Live bears were popular circus acts in the latter part of the 1800s. Naturally, the earliest of bear toys were real-looking bears standing on all 4 feet. As the toy bears increased in popularity, the sizes of the bears also increased, leading to the development of riding toys.

- Vintage bears on wheels are rare because fewer were made compared to jointed bears of the same era. The larger ones were designed as riding toys, which received harder use than jointed bears.

*12" (high), 18½" (nose to tail) by Linda Mead, 1999, Spare Bear Parts, Interlochen, Michigan*

# MATERIALS

* ⭐ ½ yd. of ¼"-pile sparse mohair fur fabric
* ⭐ 5" x 6" piece of felt for paw pads
* ⭐ 1 pair of 12 mm amber glass eyes
* ⭐ Size 3 perle cotton for nose and mouth
* ⭐ Excelsior stuffing
* ⭐ Optional
  * Firm-pack polyester stuffing
  * Wire wheel frame (See "Resources" on pages 152–153)
  * Beeswax for nose

# DIRECTIONS

*All seam allowances are ¼".*

Refer to "Getting Started" on pages 21–24 for making patterns, cutting fabric, and transferring markings. Refer to the pattern layout on page 145 before cutting pieces. Circus Bear can be made with or without the wire wheel frame.

NOTE: *Do not start or end your sewing at intersecting seam allowances. Instead, start a few stitches before and end a few stitches beyond the intersection. Backstitch at the beginning and end of all seams to lock the stiches. To do this, lift the presser foot slightly so that the fabric won't move and take several stitches in place.*

**GROOMING SEAMS:** After sewing each seam, pull fur out of seams on both wrong and right sides.

**BODY, FIRST STEP:** Pin and sew dart on each rump. Stay stitch at D and F to reinforce the belly/leg seams on the body. On one layer of fabric, begin sewing about ½" from the dot. Sew ¼" from the cut edge. Leave needle in the fabric, pivot, and take 2 stitches across the dot. Pivot again and sew about ½". Clip up to the dot, but be careful not to cut through the stitches.

**INSIDE BACK LEGS:** With right sides together, pin inside back leg to back leg on body, matching all marks. Sew the back of the leg from A to B. Sew the front of the leg from C to D. Pivot at D, realign edges, and sew from D to M. Leave bottom open for foot pad. Clip seam at ankle. Repeat for other back leg.

**INSIDE FRONT LEGS:** With right sides together, pin inside front leg to front leg on body, matching all marks. Sew from E to F. Pivot at F, realign edges, and sew from F to K. Sew from G to H. Leave bottom open for foot pad. Clip seam at ankle. Repeat for other front leg.

**FOOT PADS:** Match and pin toe mark on foot pad to toe seam of leg. Match and pin heel mark on foot pad to heel seam on leg. Pin foot pad to each side of leg. Place additional pins between these 4 pins as needed to keep raw edges of foot pad and leg even and the fullness equally distributed. With the foot pad on top, sew around foot. Refer to "Foot Pads" on page 28. Repeat for other legs. If installing wire wheel frame, cut 4 foot pads from cardboard. Lay them on sewn foot pads and trim cardboard to fit inside seam. Mark hole location for hardware as indicated in the kit instructions for a wire wheel frame.

**BODY, SECOND STEP:** Pin left and right bodies together, matching all marks. Sew from hip "Leave open" mark to A, then around the belly to P. Sew from front shoulder "Leave open" mark to Q. Make ⅛" clips along the curved seam allowance for a smoother fit when stuffing

**HEAD:** Clip ⅛" into edges of curved dart. Align edges, pin, and baste before sewing by machine, or hand sew with a tight backstitch. Pin side head pieces to chin gusset. Sew each side from S to R, with chin gusset facing up. Pin and sew head and chin seam from Q to N to S. To create a wide head, sew box-corner muzzle as described on page 29. Pin head to body, matching at Q and P. Sew around head, easing to fit as necessary. Use contrasting thread for tailor tacks to mark eye placement on outside of head.

**STUFFING:** If installing a wire wheel frame, place cardboard liners inside feet and keep holes in alignment. Use fabric glue to lightly glue cardboard in place, if desired. Do not allow foot seam allowance to come between cardboard and felt foot. Place bear on frame as described in assembly instructions included with frame. Attach wheels after face is complete. Stuff very hard with excelsior or firm-pack polyester stuffing, taking care to mold stuffing to desired shape. Close openings.

**EARS:** Pin and sew 2 ear pieces together along curved edges, leaving straight edges open. Repeat for other ear.

**FACE:** Referring to pages 35–44, install eyes, embroider nose and mouth, and attach ears. Tie off threads for eyes under chin.

**TAIL:** With right sides together, fold tail in half and sew around the large end. Clip seam allowances and turn to right side. Hand stitch small, open part of tail to rump with a ladder stitch.

**FINISHING:** Groom fur with a wire brush, especially at the seams. Decorate with felt, if desired. Give your new bear a big hug!

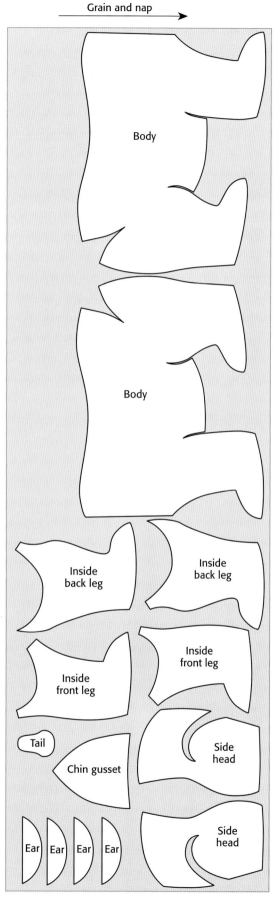

**Pattern layout**

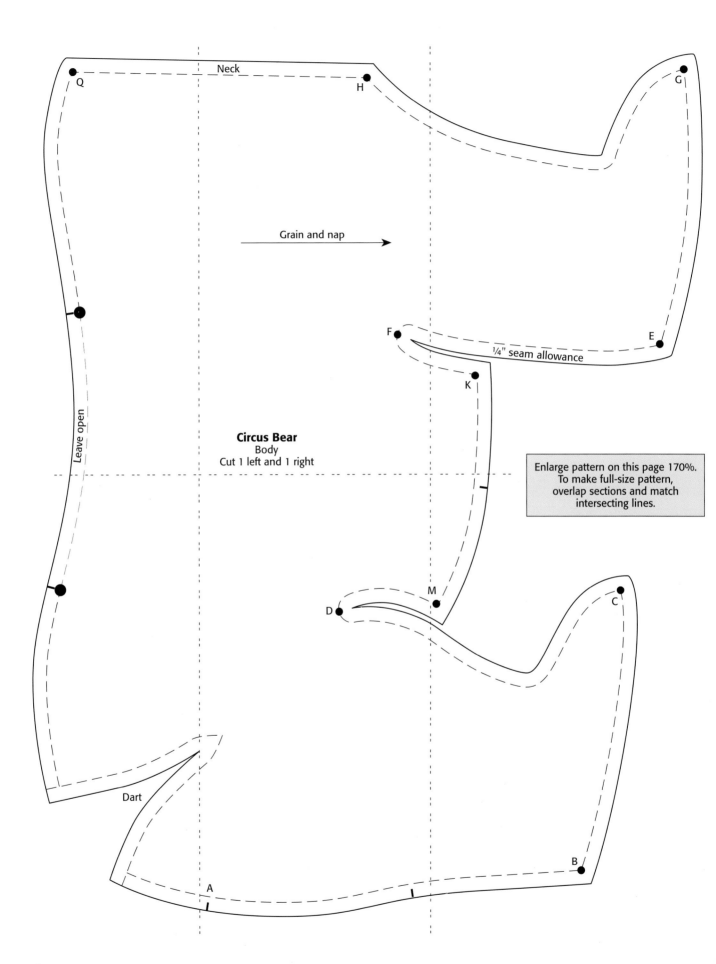

Circus Bear
Body
Cut 1 left and 1 right

Neck

Grain and nap

Leave open

¼" seam allowance

Enlarge pattern on this page 170%.
To make full-size pattern,
overlap sections and match
intersecting lines.

Dart

Q
H
G
E
F
K
M
D
C
A
B

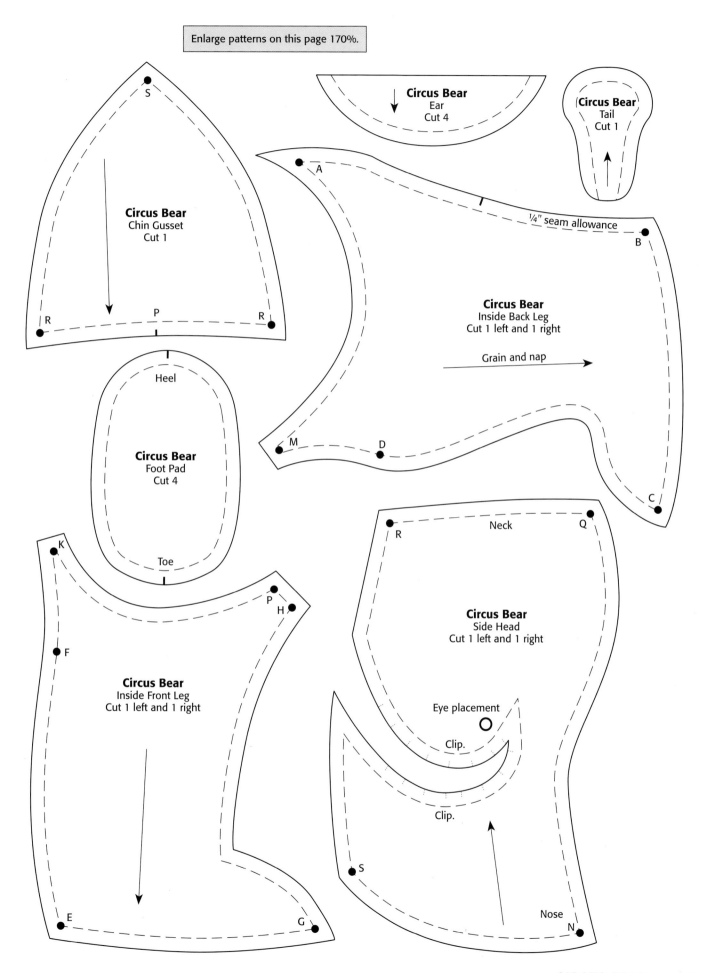

Enlarge patterns on this page 170%.

**Circus Bear**
Ear
Cut 4

**Circus Bear**
Tail
Cut 1

**Circus Bear**
Chin Gusset
Cut 1

S

R          P          R

¼" seam allowance

A

B

C

**Circus Bear**
Inside Back Leg
Cut 1 left and 1 right

Grain and nap

M          D

Heel

**Circus Bear**
Foot Pad
Cut 4

Toe

Neck

R                          Q

**Circus Bear**
Side Head
Cut 1 left and 1 right

K

P
H

F

**Circus Bear**
Inside Front Leg
Cut 1 left and 1 right

Eye placement

Clip.

Clip.

S

E                          G

Nose

N

# "SLEEPY EYES" CUBBY

🐾 🐾 *Learn how to sew in a separate muzzle and make eyelids.*

BEAR FACTS: GOOD BEARS OF THE WORLD IS A CHARITABLE ORGANIZATION, WHOSE SOLE PURPOSE IS TO PUT THE COMFORT OF A TEDDY BEAR INTO THE ARMS AND HEARTS OF EVERY TRAUMATIZED CHILD OR LONELY, FORGOTTEN ADULT IN THE WORLD. GOOD BEARS OF THE WORLD CAN AND DOES MAKE A DIFFERENCE. SEE "RESOURCES" ON PAGES 152–153 FOR CONTACT INFORMATION.

*5½" Thread Jointed Bear by Linda Mead, 1999, Spare Bear Parts, Interlochen, Michigan*

# Materials

* 4" x 8" piece of ¹/₁₆"-pile, blue mohair fur fabric
* 4" x 8" piece of ¹/₁₆"-pile, yellow mohair fur fabric
* 4" x 8" piece of ¹/₁₆"-pile, pink mohair fur fabric
* 4" x 8" piece of ¹/₁₆"-pile, green mohair fur fabric
* 2" x 3" piece of ¹/₁₆"-pile, white mohair fur fabric
* 2" square of upholstery velvet or other non-ravel fabric for eyelids
* 1 pair of 5 mm black glass eyes
* Size 8 perle cotton or blue embroidery thread for nose and mouth
* Kapok stuffing for head
* Glass bead pellets for body and limbs
* 4 buttons, ½" diameter

# Directions

*All seam allowances are ⅛".*

Refer to "Getting Started" on pages 21–24 for making patterns, cutting fabric, and transferring markings. For multicolored bear, plan cutting, sewing, and jointing so the same color pieces are not touching. Refer to photo for color guide.

**GROOMING SEAMS:** After sewing each seam, pull fur out of seams on both wrong and right sides.

**ARMS:** Pin 1 pink and 1 green arm together, matching all marks. Sew around arm, leaving an opening as marked. Repeat for other arm in blue and yellow.

**LEGS:** Pin 1 blue and 1 pink leg together, matching all marks. Sew around leg, leaving an opening as marked. Repeat for other leg in green and yellow.

**BODY:** Pin 1 front and 1 back piece together at side seam, matching all marks. Sew from neck edge to bottom corner. Repeat for remaining front and back pieces. Pin body halves together, matching all marks. Starting at "Leave open" mark on upper back, sew around hump, down front, and around bottom to "Leave open" mark on lower back.

**HEAD:** Pin head gusset to a side head piece, matching A marks. With gusset on top, sew from A to back of gusset. Repeat for other side head piece. Finish seam from end of gusset to neck edge, if necessary.

Sew darts on muzzle. Pin muzzle to head, matching all marks. Sew from B to C. Repeat for other side. Fold muzzle in half, match marks, and pin. Sew from D to C and down neck edge. Leave bottom neck edge open.

Make a box-corner nose. Fold muzzle so that the chin seam is aligned with the center of the gusset (B). The folded muzzle forms a triangle. Sew across triangle to form nose. Trim point of triangle, leaving a $^1/_{16}$" seam allowance. See "Box-Corner Muzzle" on page 29 for additional guidance.

Use contrasting thread for tailor tacks to mark eye placement on outside of head. Stuff head with kapok. Close neck opening.

EARS: Pin and sew 2 ear pieces together along curved edges, leaving straight edges open. Repeat for other ear.

STUFFING: Fill limbs and body with glass bead pellets. Close opening.

JOINTING: Referring to "Thread Jointing" on pages 52–53, attach limbs and head to body with buttons.

FACE: Referring to pages 35–44, install eyes with optional eyelids (see "Eyelids" on page 37), trim muzzle, embroider nose and mouth, and attach ears.

FINISHING: Brush fur with a wire brush, especially at the seams. Tie a ribbon around neck, if desired.  Give your new bear a hug!

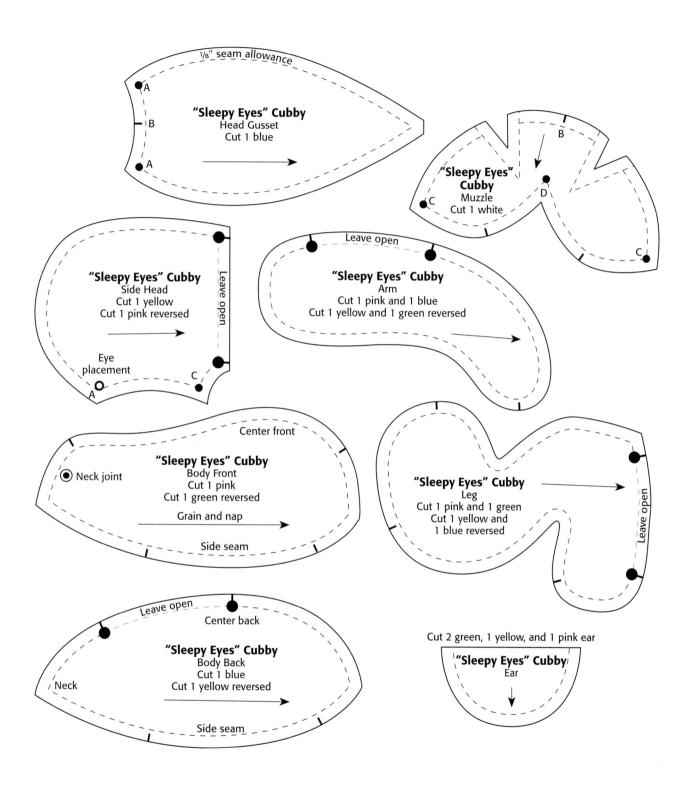

⅛" seam allowance

A

B

A

**"Sleepy Eyes" Cubby**
Head Gusset
Cut 1 blue

**"Sleepy Eyes" Cubby**
Muzzle
Cut 1 white

B

C

D

C

**"Sleepy Eyes" Cubby**
Side Head
Cut 1 yellow
Cut 1 pink reversed

Leave open

Eye placement

A

C

Leave open

**"Sleepy Eyes" Cubby**
Arm
Cut 1 pink and 1 blue
Cut 1 yellow and 1 green reversed

Center front

Neck joint

**"Sleepy Eyes" Cubby**
Body Front
Cut 1 pink
Cut 1 green reversed

Grain and nap

Side seam

**"Sleepy Eyes" Cubby**
Leg
Cut 1 pink and 1 green
Cut 1 yellow and
1 blue reversed

Leave open

Leave open

Center back

**"Sleepy Eyes" Cubby**
Body Back
Cut 1 blue
Cut 1 yellow reversed

Neck

Side seam

Cut 2 green, 1 yellow, and 1 pink ear

**"Sleepy Eyes" Cubby**
Ear

# RESOURCES

**Spare Bear Parts**
Box 56
Interlochen, MI 49643
(231) 276-7915
fax: (231) 276-7921
e-mail: Sales@SpareBear.com
web site: www.SpareBear.com
*All fabrics and other supplies used in this book are available from Spare Bear Parts, including wire wheel frame for Circus Bear on pages 142–147.*

**Andes Ribbons**
(800) 660-7830
fax: (516) 785-4370
e-mail: vic94@aol.com.
*Ribbons*

**Aztek Airbrush**
**The Testor Corporation**
620 Buckbee Street
Rockford, IL 61104-9841
Web site: www.testors.com
*Airbrush supplies*

**Badger Airbrush**
9128 W. Belmont Ave.
Franklin Park, IL 60131
(800) airbrus(h) or (800) 247-2787
Web site: www.badger-airbrush.com
*Airbrush supplies*

**Barbara's Playhouse**
25377 Huntwood Ave.
Hayward, CA 94544
(510) 785-1352
*A variety of accessories, clothing, and clothing patterns for dolls; feature over 50 different shoe styles for feet up to 4½"*

NOTE: *When using doll clothes patterns, be sure to measure the upper arm and waist and adjust if necessary.*

**JoAn Brown**
Minneapolis, MN
(763) 757-3931
e-mail: jimjoanbrown@compuserve.com
*Teddy bear supplies and classes*

**Calico Moon**
1919 State Street
Salem, OR 97301
(800) 678-7607
e-mail: calico@cyberis.net
Web site: www.boxabilities.com
*Doll/bear clothing cases and wooden needle holders*

**Clotilde Inc.**
B3000,
Louisiana, MO 63353-3000
(800) 772-2891
Web site: www.clotilde.com
*Walking foot, wooden needle holder, and other sewing accessories*

**Good Bears of the World**
Box 13097
Toledo, OH 43613-0097
(419) 531-5365
*Charitable organization*

**Linda Hartzig**
South Carolina
(704) 721-0448
fax: (704) 721-0449
e-mail: Lkheart@aol.com
*Teddy bear supplies and classes*

**Anne-Marie Lax**
**Purple Paw Productions**
(505) 281-2001
e-mail: AMHLax@aol.com
*Teddy bear supplies and classes*

**Oscar Mfg. Co.**
3929 Long Beach Blvd.
Long Beach, CA 90807
(562) 424-8780
fax: (562) 424-2270
*Ribbons*

**Renaissance Ribbons**
**The Ribbon Club**
P.O. Box 699
Oregon House, CA 95962
(530) 692-3014
e-mail: info@theribbonclub.com
Web site: www.theribbonclub.com
*Ribbons*

**Sandy Sabo**
**VitoBear Company**
(815) 477-4390
e-mail: VitoBear@aol.com
Web site: www.vitobear.com
*Teddy bear supplies and classes*

**Syndee's Crafts**
975 American Pacific Drive
Suite 201
Henderson, NV 89014
(702) 564-8118
fax: (702) 564-8178
*Impressive collection of doll/bear size furniture and accessories, including beds, dressers, wicker furniture, table and chair sets, wagons, sleds, and tricycles*

# ABOUT THE AUTHOR

LINDA'S MOTHER AND sisters always had a sewing project in progress when she was growing up. Around age four, Linda noticed embroidery was a favorite. To satisfy Linda's curiosity, her mother printed Linda's initials on a scrap of fabric and taught her how to thread the needle. When Linda stood up to show her the work, she found—much to her surprise—that she had embroidered the little patch to her dress! That's when she received her second sewing lesson, "backward sewing"! And Linda had discovered the joy of creating with a needle.

After twenty-five years of teaching adult crafts and owning a fabric store, and an additional thirteen years in television broadcast sales and management, Linda decided that she was ready for something new. She completed her first teddy bear in 1984, and it was love at first hug. As Linda became an experienced bear maker and searched for quality supplies, she soon realized that others wanted quality supplies, too. That's when the Spare Bear Parts mail-order business was born. Sharing knowledge was, and still is, at the heart of the Spare Bear Parts business. With help from husband Gordon, she has developed a traveling school to host classes. Drawing on years of teaching experience, Linda has also developed a line of patterns: The Learn Bearmaking Kit Series, the Learn Bearmaking Video, the Old Friends Kit Series, and the Designing Bear Patterns Kit and Video.

Linda currently writes the "Snip, Stitch and Stuff" column in *Soft Dolls & Animal* magazine. The column answers questions about teddy bear and soft-toy making.

# new and bestselling titles from

**Martingale™ & COMPANY**

America's Best-Loved Craft & Hobby Books™

That Patchwork Place®

America's Best-Loved Quilt Books®

## NEW RELEASES
Bear's Paw Plus
All through the Woods
American Quilt Classics
Amish Wall Quilts
Animal Kingdom CD-ROM
Batik Beauties
The Casual Quilter
Fantasy Floral Quilts
Fast Fusible Quilts
Friendship Blocks
From the Heart
Log Cabin Fever
Machine-Stitched Cathedral Stars
Magical Hexagons
Potting Shed Patchwork
Quilts from Larkspur Farm
Repliqué Quilts
Successful Scrap Quilts
    from Simple Rectangles

## APPLIQUÉ
Artful Album Quilts
Artful Appliqué
Colonial Appliqué
Red and Green: An Appliqué Tradition
Rose Sampler Supreme

## BABY QUILTS
Easy Paper-Pieced Baby Quilts
Even More Quilts for Baby: Easy as ABC
More Quilts for Baby: Easy as ABC
Play Quilts
The Quilted Nursery
Quilts for Baby: Easy as ABC

## HOLIDAY QUILTS
Christmas at That Patchwork Place
Holiday Collage Quilts
Paper Piece a Merry Christmas
A Snowman's Family Album Quilt
Welcome to the North Pole

## LEARNING TO QUILT
Basic Quiltmaking Techniques for:
    Borders and Bindings
    Divided Circles
    Hand Appliqué
    Machine Appliqué
    Strip Piecing
The Joy of Quilting
The Simple Joys of Quilting
Your First Quilt Book (or it should be!)

## PAPER PIECING
50 Fabulous Paper-Pieced Stars
For the Birds
Paper Piece a Flower Garden
Paper-Pieced Bed Quilts
Paper-Pieced Curves
A Quilter's Ark
Show Me How to Paper Piece

## ROTARY CUTTING
101 Fabulous Rotary-Cut Quilts
365 Quilt Blocks a Year Perpetual Calendar
Around the Block Again
Biblical Blocks
Creating Quilts with Simple Shapes
Flannel Quilts
More Fat Quarter Quilts
More Quick Watercolor Quilts
Razzle Dazzle Quilts

## SCRAP QUILTS
Nickel Quilts
Scrap Frenzy
Scrappy Duos
Spectacular Scraps

## CRAFTS
The Art of Stenciling
Baby Dolls and Their Clothes
Creating with Paint
The Decorated Kitchen
The Decorated Porch
A Handcrafted Christmas
Painted Chairs
Sassy Cats

## KNITTING & CROCHET
Too Cute!
Clever Knits
Crochet for Babies and Toddlers
Crocheted Sweaters
Fair Isle Sweaters Simplified
Irresistible Knits
Knit It Your Way
Knitted Shawls, Stoles, and Scarves
Knitted Sweaters for Every Season
Knitting with Novelty Yarns
Paintbox Knits
Simply Beautiful Sweaters
Simply Beautiful Sweaters for Men
The Ultimate Knitter's Guide

Our books are available at bookstores and your favorite craft, fabric and yarn retailers. If you don't see the title you're looking for, visit us at www.martingale-pub.com or contact us at:

## 1-800-426-3126
International: 1-425-483-3313
Fax: 1-425-486-7596
E-mail: info@martingale-pub.com

For more information and a full list of our titles, visit our Web site or call for a free catalog.